THE CREATIVE CHILD

THE CREATIVE CHILD

How to Encourage the Natural Creativity
of Your Preschooler

by
Stephen Lehane, Ed. D.

A SPECTRUM BOOK

PRENTICE-HALL, INC., Englewood Cliffs, New Jersey 07632

Library of Congress Cataloging in Publication Data

Lehane, Stephen.
The creative child.

(A Spectrum Book)
Bibliography: p.
Includes index.
1. Creative ability in children.   2. Education,
Preschool. I. Title
BF723.C7L43   155.4'13   79-26593
ISBN 0-13-189118-9
ISBN 0-13-189100-6 pbk.

Stephen Lehane teaches at Duke University and is the author
of *Help Your Baby Learn* published by Prentice-Hall. He is
also the author of more than two dozen films.

Design and Production by
Susan Alger Walrath
THE BOOK DEPARTMENT
52 Roland Street
Charlestown, Massachusetts 02129

10 9 8 7 6 5 4 3 2 1

Printed in the United States of America

PRENTICE-HALL INTERNATIONAL, INC., London
PRENTICE-HALL OF AUSTRALIA PTY. LIMITED, Sydney
PRENTICE-HALL OF CANADA, LTD., Toronto
PRENTICE-HALL OF INDIA PRIVATE LIMITED, New Delhi
PRENTICE-HALL OF JAPAN, INC., Tokyo
PRENTICE-HALL OF SOUTHEAST ASIA PTE. LTD., Singapore
WHITEHALL BOOKS LIMITED, Wellington, New Zealand

TO

SMEDGE
GOOGY
EXIE

CONTENTS

I
THE DREAMER STAGE 14
2-4 Years Old

II
THE POET STAGE 80
3-5 Years Old

ACTIVITIES

III
THE INVENTOR STAGE   132
4-6 Years Old

ACTIVITIES

IV
CREATIVE ENVIRONMENTS 190

PREFACE

This preface is drawn from a number of remarks and comments made by the author's three children while this book was being written.

When Daddy started this book he asked fifteen thousand, two hundred and eighty-three million, four hundred and seven of the dumbest questions you ever heard: "What color is this? How many fingers do you have? What letter comes after *r*? Point to your nose. Where's up? Can you make a square?" He sounded like Big Bird but wasn't half as funny.

Then one day he blew up. The pressure had gotten to him. All his questions had added up to nothing but one fat zero. What finally made him crack was drilling Erin on her math facts: "If one and one are two, and two and two are four, then what's one plus four?"

"That's not fair," Erin responded, "You answered all the easy ones yourself!"

He flung all his zillions of note cards in the air and screamed, "These kids are totally illogical, but they're outsmarting me at every turn."

Now Daddy was on the right track. We were smart about certain things. Rather than asking us about things we didn't know or care about, he began spending time with us playing cowboys and Indians, watching "The Three Stooges" on Saturday morning, and helping us write to Santa Claus.

We always had the right answers; it was Daddy who had the wrong questions. He once called our answers imaginative. We called it having fun. Whatever it's called, it stopped Daddy and made him write this book on what we do best. He finally called it creativity.

Christopher, Erik, and Erin Lehane
Lenox, Massachusetts
1979

INTRODUCTION

How good are you at spotting genius? Could you name the young poet who, upon seeing a sunset, remarked, "I'd love to go for a ride in the rays and go to bed in sheets made of clouds"?

Would you believe it was a four-year old? Spend a day in a nursery school and you'll be dazzled at how easily such poetic, imaginative, and fanciful creations flow from young children. It is their native tongue; yet for grown-ups, such creativity requires great effort. It's more than coincidence that when topflight places like Harvard and MIT want to instill creativity in students, they focus on metaphorical, allegorical, and other forms of intuitive thought common to the young child. In his book on developing imagination in businessmen, Gordon (1961) states that creativity requires "relearning on an adult level techniques which were natural in the intuitive vision of childhood." Along the same vein,

Dr. James Wiesner, president of MIT, writes, "Although analogy and metaphor are out of place in formal reasoning, they may turn out to be dominant in the intuitive, sometimes illogical, and initially random processes of creatively scanning and searching for new connections and clues" (Kagan 1967).

Why do adults have to be retaught to think like children? Why does the flame of imagination dim with age? My theory is that the years between two and six mark the crucial period in which creativity develops and, if not cultivated then, creativity is very hard to rekindle later in life.

Unfortunately, virtually everything written about early childhood treats it as some "pre" or preparational stage. Even the term *preschool*, used to designate our early years of life, implies a grooming period for some big event to come. It's as if the inventiveness and fantasy of these early years had no inherent value. Yet Einstein credited the discovery of relativity to a fantasy he had of traveling through space on a beam of light. Einstein does not stand alone. According to A.C. Crombie (1952), the noted historian of science, hundreds of scientific breakthroughs have been sparked by whims, superstitions, and other forms of magical thinking. Though such thinking plays a big part in creativity, it is only half the picture. To turn any fanciful idea into something that's useful demands a lot of hard work and sound reasoning, not just dreaming. Apparently what creative persons can do that others can't is to travel easily between their dream worlds and the world of fact. Barron (1963) recognizes this when he comments, "The effectively original person may be characterized above all by an ability to regress very far for the moment while being able to quite rapidly return to a high degree of rationality, bringing with him the imaginative and fantastic fruits of his regression." In short, any creative achievement, be it in science or art, ultimately represents the union of imagination and reason. The purpose of this book is to show how to stimulate both processes without playing up one at the cost of the other.

Today most early childhood education is geared toward developing the child's ability to reason, which, in comparison to an adult's ability, is, of course, undeveloped. This shoring up of the undeveloped nature of the child has always been the mission of early childhood education. It is evident in the pioneering efforts of Pestalozzi, Froebel, and Montessori, as well as in our more recent Headstart campaign. All these educational efforts have been aimed at children whose development has suffered the ravages of war, poverty, pestilence, neglect, broken homes, and uprooted families.

Unquestionably curricula bearing the stamp of Pestalozzi, Froebel, Montessori, and Headstart have all been noble and humanistic undertakings. Yet they have left the field of early childhood education with a focus on treating the troubled or undeveloped aspects of youngsters, rather than their strengths. Today we seem to have forgotten the idea that every child, regardless of race, color, or background, has talents. At the turn of the century, however, this idea was one of the guideposts of education: "All children unless they be idiots have productive or creative imagination in some measure" (Burnham 1892). Unfortunately, the traditional viewpoint of early childhood education prevailed until the field was graced by the contributions of two great figures, Freud and Piaget. Freud felt that adult creativity was but a continuation of childhood fantasies and that the key to creative actions was regression, or sliding back into one's early stage of play and fantasy (Kris 1952). Like Freud, Piaget (1928) found the preschooler's mind rich with invention and imagination; he established a whole stage of intellectual development for this period, which he called "intuitive thinking." According to Piaget (1952), intelligence has two functions: inventing and verifying. "The first partakes of imagination and the second alone is purely logical."

Though intelligence appears to be a partnership between imagination and logic, educators have generally ignored this relationship. Dr. Lawrence Kubie (1958), writing for the American Academy of Arts and Science, warned that schools are too formal and rational, a condition that hampers the *preconscious*—his term for the part of the mind where fantasy and imagination are housed. In Kubie's words, "Educational research today should attempt to protect the preconscious functions in all education but especially in education for creativity."

The first step in protecting creativity in young children is to try to see the world from their perspective. That perspective often appears mixed up and can require a lot of detective work before things are sorted out. Such was the case in the "string bean" incident, which grew out of an argument between my two boys over the nature of God. Erik's insistence that God was a "string bean" threw Christopher into a convulsive rage. After things simmered down, Erik seemed to be changing his mind when he said, "You're right Chris. God ain't just no string bean. He's a super bean like in Jack's beanstalk."

Before Christopher could get to his little brother's jugular, I stepped in and started questioning Erik, only to find that he had learned about the "string bean" from Sunday school. Things then began to click in my mind. Erik was apparently saying "string bean," when what he really meant to say was "Supreme Being." Never having heard that phrase before, Erik simply connected it with something he knew. But string bean was too dull to carry the majesty befitting a deity, so Erik made yet another association and came up with the all-powerful and mysterious "super bean" of "Jack and the Beanstalk."

Erik's zigzag line of reasoning is known as *thinking by association*. It is the basic way that kids, as well as creative adults, think. Einstein described it as "combinatory associations or the playing around with different combinations of ideas" (Ghiselin 1952). Thinking by association triggers metaphorical and allegorical concepts—like Erin's definition of ice: "water going to sleep for the winter." It is also a style of thinking that has been responsible for many breakthroughs in science. Neils Bohr formulated the physics principle of complementarity from his metaphorical view of love and justice, while Alexander Graham Bell's invention of the telephone was guided by an analogy based on the bones and parts of the human ear.

According to most researchers, the ability to make associations is a key ingredient in creativity (Wallach and Kagan 1965).

Virtually every test of creativity measures the number and uniqueness of such associations (Torrance 1962). Interestingly, Getzel and Jackson (1962) discovered that the ability to form associations is not linked to high intelligence. It appears that an average IQ is sufficient for creativity. However, as Wallach and Kagan concluded, neither associations nor intelligence tells the whole story: the way that individuals use time to cultivate their ideas is also essential to creativity.

From the testimony of artists, scientists, and researchers, it seems that all creative undertakings involve the elements of time, associations, and intelligence. These elements work themselves out in at least three stages (Hughes 1963): *incubation*, when time is spent concocting millions of ideas; *illumination*, the "flash point" when ideas are brought together in original and unique associations; *verification*, when intelligence is applied to making these associations workable in the real world.

Young children go through similar creative stages.

I-THE DREAMER (2-4 years old)

At this stage, the child has just discovered the marvelous workings of the mind: an unbarred imagination and an ability to dream up hundreds of unconnected thoughts. There are no limits to the child's dreams because they are rarely applied to the real world. Children at this age are content to allot all their time to stirring up a jumble of ideas, impressions, and images, which they then lock away in their dream worlds for private use only.

II-THE POET (3-5 years old)

At this point, thoughts flow at a more manageable pace, which makes it easier for children to see associations among their ideas. However, they grasp their associations on an intuitive level—that is, they understand and express them only in terms of analogies, similes, and other poetic forms. The poet has not yet reached the stage where he can put into words the poetic images that are flooding his mind.

III-THE INVENTOR (4-6 years old)

There is little growth in creativity until children see their poetic ideas in need of refinement. During the second stage, the child came up with analogies to solve real problems. At this third stage, the child, like an inventor, tries to turn the analogies into real ideas that are practicable in the outside world. This demands hard work, intelligence, and a general stick-to-itiveness.

These stages of creativity parallel the work of Piaget (1926) and Erikson (1963). While Piaget charts early cognition as passing through three stages—autistic, egocentric, and sociocentric—Erikson maintains that personality evolves through the periods of autonomy, initiative, and industry. There are some interesting overlaps between the stages of these two theorists:

Autistic-autonomy: The child is wrapped up in his own world, much like the dreamer.

Egocentric-initiative: The child tries to step out of his world and communicate but is hampered for many reasons, not unlike those factors that check the poet.

Sociocentric-industry: At this stage, the child is pouring all his energy into adapting to the real world, as is the inventor.

Although these stages roughly correspond with certain years, they do spill over into different age groups, as shown in the following table:

Age	% of Time in Dreamer-Autistic-Autonomy Stage	% of Time in Poet-Egocentric-Initiative Stage	% of Time in Inventor-Sociocentric-Industry Stage
2-4	50	25	25
3-5	25	50	25
4-6	25	25	50

Though the basic idea of this book is that these early years are the seat of creativity the stages just mentioned do continue throughout life. The dreamer predominates again roughly between seven and fourteen years of age; the poet between fifteen and thirty; and, finally, the inventor from middle age on. Whether one can extract all the creativity from these later stages depends on how well creativity was developed during the earlier years.

Although everything done during the earlier stages is obviously not creative, the point of *The Creative Child* is to familiarize you with those behaviors that do contribute to creative thinking. However, before going any further, one point should be made clear: Children do not display their creativity in the same way as adults. Don't expect to see instant signs of genius. Rather, be on the lookout for unusual ways of dealing with everyday problems: youngsters combat loneliness with imaginary friends; overcome death with fantasies of reincarnation; adjust to pain and loss with make-believe figures, such as the tooth fairy; and let out their frustrations by throwing temper tantrums—it's better than developing an ulcer. Typically, we gloss over these behaviors as being nothing more than childish little antics. But the truth of the matter is that they reflect intuitive and wildly imaginative minds running at full throttle. If creativity is cultivated during the early years, these antics are soon outgrown, and the mind can continue to send out imaginative sparks that eventually catch fire. Although your child may not develop into another Einstein or Beethoven, he or she nonetheless has a flexible mind capable of coping with life in a rational, as well as a highly imaginative, manner.

Unlike other approaches that use art (Hendrick 1975), brainstorming, and rewards (Torrance 1970) to bring out creativity as if it were lost, hidden, or as hard to extract as teeth, this book maintains that creativity is all around the young. However, one cannot stand back waiting for it to develop. To do so would result in permissiveness or a form of free thinking that only produces unreal dreamers. There's no getting around it: One has to take an active part in bringing up children. This book describes the many activities you can engage in with children that foster their creative potential. These activities give young children confidence in their intuitive thinking; and such confidence is crucial because, as we saw earlier, educators and, for that matter, adults in general tend to gloss over the importance of this early intuitive thought. If there's one thing researchers have found that separates the creative from the noncreative person, it is the creative person's confidence and motivation to use unusual forms of thinking in dealing with the world (Kagan 1967).

Later, with the acquisition of logic, children have two ways of dealing with reality: one, logical; the other, creative. Both have their place and, what may be more important, both have their time. Unfortunately, most educators try to cultivate logical thinking during the preschool years (incidentally, without much success), and then when logic is finally obtained in adolescence, these same educators cry over their student's lack of creativity. Ironically, it is often this very effort to instill logic in young minds that forces creativity underground.

It's easy to fall into the trap of using logic with young children. If anything, they lure us into it with their great achievement, the ability to speak. We assume that if they can talk as we do, they can also think as we do, which is about as reliable as believing that right after a baby takes her first step she's ready to run with us. While the use of language obviously marks the start of adult reasoning, it less obviously also marks the start of something just as critical: the beginning of the generation gap. Although we've come to expect this breakdown in communication with adolescents, we usually don't realize that the gap has been building up for years before this time. Take the story of three-year-old Tony, who, upon hearing that he and his family were flying to their vacation, threw himself into a tantrum and his home into chaos. There was no reasoning with him. Consulting with doctors did little good until this poor tyke, kicking, screaming, and flailing like a caged animal, arrived at the airport only to see that they were going by plane and not by jumping off a building and flying themselves.

If Tony had been thirteen, this particular misunderstanding would have been noted as a glaring example of the generation gap. But the gap doesn't start with teenagers; it's set off in the toddler years and then spreads until it reaches a head at adolescence, at which point it's often too late to start patching things up. The time to avert an unbridgeable gap is when your child is still young. Like anything else, it's easier to change in the beginning before ironclad habit takes hold.

One way to circumvent the generation gap is to be open to the idea that youngsters have something important to say, even if they do not always convey it in adult terms. So, let your guard drop and slip into their magical world of windships and dragons. You have nothing to lose and a world to gain. And the passport for this trip—*The Creative Child*—is in your hands.

Today we're too keen on teaching youngsters about our world without paying any attention to their world. Learning to classify and seriate will come naturally to most children. What they need from us is assurance that their dreams and imaginations won't be choked off by too early a diet of logic and reason.

This is not a tract against reason. Rather, it is a plea that we keep a foot in both camps and especially that we keep alive the child's gift of dreaming, without which all creativity stalls. To paraphrase G. B. Shaw, "The reasonable man adapts himself to his surroundings. The dreamer persists in trying to adapt the surroundings to himself.... Progress hinges on the latter."

HOW
TO USE
THIS BOOK

To a scientist, they were but a handful of igneous stratified sediments, but to Erin, pebbles were "crumbs of the earth."

In a similar vein, many grown-ups see children as nothing more than half-baked adults, while others picture them as pint-sized Picassos. Take your choice; but whether you're talking about children or rocks, the view you have of them will definitely color the way you treat them and the manner in which they respond to you.

You will only be able to see children as creative if you really believe they are. In essence, this is the business of this book: to show you how to discover and encourage the creativity that's lurking in your child's everyday behavior. Hang up your old notions of young children. You're not going to hear anything about prelogical development or states of readiness. The youngster from two to six isn't waiting for something to happen; he or she is already engaged in the most creative part of life. Follow me through the wild and imaginative worlds of my three children, Christopher, Erik, and Erin, and then use this book to explore your own child's world of fantasy.

QUESTIONS AND ANSWERS

To understand children's creativity, you must first be able to pick their brains with questions that are important to them. This book contains many such questions. These questions are based on the typical daily activities of three young children and cover everything from concerns about Santa Claus to playing cops and robbers. Once you have fired questions, the trick becomes how to interpret the youngster's responses. According to my wife, Mary, that's where the "third ear" comes into play. If you're like most of us, this imaginative listening device went deaf just at the time you stopped believing in the tooth fairy. The first step in restoring this ear is knowing when the youngster is "putting you on" with her answers and when she's on the up-and-up.

Children basically meet adult questions with five classic comebacks:

1. Shooting from the hip: This response is the pure whimsy you get if you keep pestering the child.
2. Joking: The youngster makes up something she considers funny because your probes are long and boring. Often, it will be a nonsense word that rhymes with a term you've just used in a question.
3. Feeding you a line: You get the answer you might have expected because your question suggested it. (For example, "Who made

the sun?" implies some kind of a person manufacturing a product. A better question would be, "What is the sun?")

4. Thinking on one's feet: Here the question catches the child completely off guard, and he has to come up with a clever, if not unique, response. The more time you spend with children, the easier it becomes to dream up such questions.

5. Maintaining silence: This response is usually reserved for the armchair expert who is so out of touch with real children that his questions draw only blanks.

ACTIVITIES AND DIARY

The questions you'll be asking center around the activities that are presented in the next three chapters. The point of each activity is noted in the "objective" at the beginning of each activity section. Each of these three chapters deals with a different stage of creativity. Since there is some overlap among the stages, it's a good idea to start with the "Dreamer" and then move to the "Poet" and "Inventor" chapters. The final chapter, "Creative Environments," includes many pointers on how to reorganize part of the school day so that it's more in step with the imaginative development of children.

Whatever you do, don't become upset if your youngster botches some of the activities. Her other answers may be more creative than the ones expected. Don't even keep score of the right and wrong answers. If you're going to record anything, jot down the imaginative things your child did or said in a situation similar to the one I describe for that particular activity. You'll have plenty of room to make notes in the diary provided after each activity.

Finally, take your time and don't rush your youngster through any of these activities. Remember Einstein didn't speak until he was three, which apparently didn't hurt him a bit. If anything, he considered it a blessing: "My intellectual development was slow and so I didn't start to think about space and time until I was already grown up. Consequently, I went into these problems more thoroughly than a child would"—obviously the understatement of the century (Stockton 1979).

CHAPTER

I

THE
DREAMER
STAGE

2-4 YEARS OLD

Robert Louis Stevenson swore it inspired *Dr. Jekyll and Mr. Hyde.* Coleridge never tired of telling the world how it sparked his great poem *Kubla Khan,* while Kekulé, one of the leading chemists of all times, claimed that his discovery of the benzene rings sprang straight from it. What was this magical "it," this creative super power? None other than daydreaming!

On hearing this claim, one young mother cracked, "If you're just half right, then our Jeffery's another Einstein. He always seems to be up in the clouds in some twilight zone. Yet nothing ever comes of it." And nothing ever really will, because Jeff's brand of daydreaming is merely an escape valve, a trance for wish fulfillment. Though both forms of daydreaming reach their peak between the ages of two and four, the creative type of daydreaming continues throughout life. Dr. Noam Chomsky of MIT, one of today's top linguists, would never leave home without it. He writes, "I dream about all my problems. But I wouldn't call daydreaming any different from my other lab work" (Cohen 1977).

Such dreaming is but the first leg in any creative process. It's the birthplace of all our ideas. It is the point at which we sit back as onlookers and allow our thoughts to think for themselves. Bertrand

Russell believes that "it's a non-thinking time when the subconscious is free to go on a creative shopping spree and randomly sift through the different departments of the brain." For dreamers like Russell, contemplating ideas is life's most exciting activity. These ideas need not be acted upon. Action is saved for other stages. Few grown-ups are as lucky as Russell or Chomsky; most of us have forgotten how to empty dreams of their creative potential. Unquestionably, children are more adept at this than adults. But the question is: How do children pull it off? Being children, they're not going to tip their hands just for the asking. To get them to open up, you're going to have to turn to some pretty sophisticated maneuvers—such as rearranging furniture!

I stumbled across the furniture idea completely by accident while painting Erin's room. Once the walls dried, she wouldn't stop pestering me until I had pushed together her bed and dresser to form a nice cozy nook. That was the last time I saw her for a week. She turned hermit or, at best, a boarder who rarely came down for meals. Enough was enough. I snuck up to her room expecting to catch her secretly doing something outrageous, only to find my little girl all curled up in her private niche. Clearly she was hypnotized by the scene outside her window: a shower of brightly colored autumn leaves. She had the concentration of a zoom lens. Trying to inch my way into her private world, I made some small talk about how beautiful the leaves were. Suddenly her head swiveled around like a gun turret and between clenched teeth, in a very measured tone, she said, "Daddy, let's see if we can be as quiet as a leaf turning colors."

I should have guessed something like this might have happened. For most youngsters, and Erin was by no means an exception, private nooks cast spells that set the mind free to dream. Young children don't stand alone in this matter. Samuel Johnson, Carlyle, and Proust never lifted a pen unless they were as snug as bugs in their own out-of-the-way, soundproof writing dens. Such shelters supply creative persons with the peace of mind they need to sort out their thoughts.

Whereas ordinary people handle information in nice, neat logical bundles, the dreamer is hit with a barrage of unconnected images, like flashbacks in a movie. Unable to handle this overload, the dreamer shifts to the subconscious and goes on the "creative shopping spree" described by Bertrand Russell. The images seen by the mind's eye are called *eidetic visions*. Obviously they're not the bread and butter of our thinking, which is logic. At best, eidetic images have been found in less than 10 percent of the adult population; yet over 60 percent of children under seven feel quite at home with this form of thinking. According to Professor Paul Torrance, education's foremost spokesman on creativity, this is but another sign in the decline of creativity with age (Torrance 1970).

How do you stop this slippage? For openers, don't hound the dreamer. Put aside a special spot where she can be alone to sort out her images. Without such privacy, the dreamer turns out like Jeff, snatching every private moment for dreaming of wish fulfill-ment. However, there are times when the child tires of privacy and is ripe for outside stimulation. At these times the child is operating as a public dreamer. As such, he's no longer anchored to his own closed world of private ideas. Rather, the untold hundreds of little things that are happening all around him have become the chief source of his ideas and creativity. This openness to external matters has led to some major breakthroughs, not the least of which was Alexander Flemming's discovery of one of the wonder drugs of all time. When a speck of dust threatened to spoil an experiment, Flemming's openness and curiosity led him to ana-lyze the speck, which eventually turned out to be penicillin.

The public dreamer is so hungry for stimulation that she soaks up any odds and ends or offhand comments like a sponge. Everything is taken in and let to simmer on the back burner of the subconscious. This stimulation begins to bubble over and is expressed through physical actions in games, play, art, or other bodily expressions. Typically, a dreamer might say, "There's something alive inside of me. I can't say it but I can dance it." Once the subconscious plays out its dreams publicly, the cycle begins all over again with the child returning to dream about these experiences in private. It is during the private cycle that the experiences are made ready for the poet to communicate.

Though the dreamer leaves little doubt in anyone's mind that she wants privacy, she does little to let you know that she's going public. If anything she's a bit boring and shy—a wallflower. It's like pulling teeth to get her to interact with you. But if you don't make the effort, most of her creative energies will be spent on ideas to meet private needs.

Alexander Graham Bell is an example of a private dreamer. His invention of the telephone stemmed from a deep concern over deafness in his family. On the other hand, Thomas Edison, who was hard of hearing, still managed to parlay his creativity into hundreds of inventions, among them the phonograph, microphone, mimeograph, light bulb, motion picture, and the first talkies. The difference between the two men was not so much a matter of inborn talent as the amount of attention and extra stimulation each received during their public spurts of dreaming.

Obviously if your child doesn't have the creative ingredients to start with, you are not going to whip her into a Bell or an Edison. Yet whatever special spark or gift she does have can be shaped into either private or broad creativity, depending on the way she's treated during this phase of life.

Although the poetic and inventive phases hog the limelight for the next few years, you haven't completely washed your hands of the dreamer. The dreamer lingers on in the shadows of the next two stages and makes a strong comeback just at the time the youngster starts school. From then until the early teens, dreaming once again colors most of the child's creative undertakings. During its rerun, dreaming covers roughly the same span as Freud's stage of latency. In the latency stage, the characteristics of the dreamer tend to be more readily observable:

> *Daydreaming:* Eidetic images return and are contemplated but not communicated.

Shyness: The dreamer seeks privacy.

Idle wishing: If privacy is not provided, dreaming becomes mere wish fulfillment.

Crisis of broad vs. private creativity: Special attention during bouts of public dreaming leads to broad applications of talent, while a lack of such attention tends to yield private forms of creativity.

1

Little People

OBJECTIVE:
IDENTIFYING A STAGE
OF ARTIFICIALISM IN
THE DREAMER

Did I mention that my kids are orphans? Legend has it, at least from the snatches of conversation I have been able to glean, that their real parents, under the cover of a terrible storm, sought to flee from the Land of the Little People but were "smucked" by the Stonemen. But that's only the half of it. Whenever Christopher, Erik, or Erin have had enough, when the rat race of play groups,

"Sesame Street," and *Dr. Seuss* has become too much, they pack up their dreams and slip away back to the Little People. There they shed their humdrum identities and become Smedge, Googy, and Exie, the make-believe supreme rulers of this fantasy land.

Little People may appear to be a child's version of the classic escape valve from the pressures of everyday life. But don't jump the gun. There's more to this than meets the eye. For openers, the Land of the Little People is an unusual example of children's sharing one dream together. Because the dream is shared, it cuts through all the stages of creativity. To keep pace with the children as they move through the different stages of creativity, the fantasy of the Little People can even create its own language, which advances to match the children's development. One of my favorite Little People words is the polysyllabic term *pleditrants*, which, loosely translated, means all the spooky feelings one gets from dark places. Similar terms were used to fill notes, letters, maps, and sets of directions my youngsters left for each other. It is amazing, but nonetheless a fact, that they were far less literary in their real worlds than in this dream world.

Not all Little People are literary. There is a definite pecking order, at the bottom of which squat the Mingys. They are a dull and lazy lot made up of discarded toys—rusty tin soldiers, broken dolls, lumpy stuffed animals, and the like. The Mingys are considered a jinx; they are the Little People's scapegoats. Hence, it is always open season on them. Fortunately little blood is ever spilled in this land because no one ever lifts a finger without first clearing their actions with Captain Cunningham, the Little People's resident witch doctor. You see, everything in the Land of the Little People hinges on superstition.

Superstition is one form of *artificialism*, which is a type of broad thinking that holds that the whole world is controlled by some great hero, or god. You can control the world, make wishes come true, and so on, if you know how to contact these superpowers. Basically this contact is established by spouting magic words and following certain rituals or superstitions.

Being a rational college professor, I was put off by such thinking. But gradually I learned that it was one key to opening up the dreamer's world. In discussing superstitions with my children, I learned more about their feelings, thoughts, and perceptions than I did from any textbook.

Once you get into superstitions, they will act as a wedge and provide an opening through which you can get in touch with your child's dream world. Here are some superstitions to get the ball rolling: black cats; spilling salt and throwing it over your shoulder; seven years of bad luck from breaking a mirror; four-leaf clovers; walking under ladders; a rabbit's foot; horseshoes; unlucky number thirteen; itchy palms; putting a shirt on backward; and a howling dog.

Ask your child what some of these superstitions mean. Explain the ones she's never heard. Does she believe in them? Which ones work and which ones don't? Why do some work and others not work? What are some of her superstitions? Ask where superstitions come from.

DIARY:

2

Mud
Pies

OBJECTIVE:
OBSERVING THE
DREAMER EXPRESSING
UNACCEPTABLE BEHAVIOR

Last winter my aunt invited us to spend a week in Florida at her place on the Gulf Coast. Among other things, our kids love to scoop up wet beach sand and fashion all types of mud pies. One afternoon a very proper Bostonian matron came dripping out of the surf. Half-exhausted, she plopped herself squarely down upon two of Erik's masterpieces. In a typical kid's whisper, audible across the beach, Erik whimpered, "She stole my pies!" Enraged, the blue blood rose from the beach, ramrod straight, and marched away in a huff. It took every last ounce of restraint for Erik to hold back the laughter that was on the verge of explosion. Suddenly it was too much and the wave of hysteria broke through, sending him into convulsions. Rolling on the ground, he managed to point out to his brother and sister the two mud pies that had been mashed to the seat of the lady's swimsuit.

This episode was not lost on my kids' imaginations for they spent the rest of the morning huddled together, hatching secret plans for kneading, shaping, and stamping out mud pies that looked like you know what—BMs. Interestingly enough, once the BMs rolled off the production line, they were immediately destroyed. Obviously they were not meant for the eyes of the public. Here was a perfect example of the dreamer moving through the cycle of private to public and then back to private world.

Mud and its cousins, clay and plasticene, are well suited for the private world of the dreamer. They allow him to produce contraband, to express forbidden images in concrete form. The contraband often represents objects that are off limits to the child. These forbidden items include everything from mud feces and sexual objects to little clay candies and toy guns. In this way children get around everyday taboos against eating too many sweets and playing violent games. In short, the clay or mud lets the child get his secret dreams out in the open.

The greatest pleasure the dreamer gets from his sculpturing is not so much the finished product as the handling and experiencing of a forbidden object. Molding materials lend themselves to this purpose. They are quick to the touch and can be easily reshaped to meet any new dream that pops into the dreamer's head. Also, being as soft as putty, they can be punched, torn, and squeezed without causing any harm and yet still serve as an outlet for the dreamer's private frustrations. Beyond this, there is the basic, if not primitive, sensory experience that comes from digging our fingers into mud or clay and working it with our hands. Such an experience triggers the dreamer's memory and jogs his eidetic images into action. In a sense, clay acts as an instant replay. One way to stimulate eidetic images while the child is playing with clay is to supply him with some mementos of past experiences: pictures, airplane tickets, sea shells, clothes used on vacations, Christmas records, birthday cards, and so on.

Which mementos cause the dreamer to make the most sculptures? Are the sculptures contraband? What types of sculptures are used for letting off steam or for punching and hitting?

DIARY: _____

3

Cops
and
Robbers

OBJECTIVE:
OBSERVING THE DEVELOPMENT
OF TRUTH AND JUSTICE IN
THE DREAMER

Christmas morning at the Lehane's house was something else. I'd love to say it was a family scene right out of a Norman Rockwell painting, but it was in fact more like a family feud right out of the era of the Hatfields and McCoys. Instead of "Peace on earth, good will toward men," what rang through our house was "Bang-bang, you're dead. Fifty bullets in your head!" What it meant was that the kids had opened their presents, grown quickly tired of their new toys, and had now piled the gift boxes around the tree, making a fort or jail for playing cops and robbers, cowboys and Indians, and other versions of that age-old favorite—playing "guns." Even though toy guns had not been given for Christmas, it would be only a matter of time before my fishing rod became a rifle and Mary's mixing bowl a helmet. It was no different this year than in years past, when the kids did in fact receive six-shooters and holsters from old St. Nick.

"Guns for Christmas presents!" Believe it or not, playing guns may be one of the most moral games children ever play. Forget the experts on this one; they are (excuse the pun) dead wrong. In addition, most youngsters can outwit parental crusades against guns. One couple was so brainwashed that they even banned water pistols, whereupon their children began chewing their sand-wiches into little guns which they then fired at each other. Another parent, a diehard hunter with a den full of shotguns and stuffed trophies, put a total freeze on war toys. Since it is what parents practice rather than what they preach that really sinks into the child, it would seem highly likely that the children in this family will soon be following in their father's footsteps.

Toy guns are *not* bad for children. You and I are living proof of it. If your childhood was anything like mine, there was a time when you never missed a day without drilling someone or knocking over a bank. Yet we didn't end up behind bars. Playing guns is normal. It's kid stuff. It's part of growing up. In fact, it's a tonic for the soul.

Few activities are governed with more concern for justice, morality, or a stricter adherence to rules. When Christopher "pow-pows" Erik, who then bites the dust, Erik is operating from blind faith. How does he know Christopher got him? He has nothing to go on but Chris's word. What is even more interesting is that when Erik shouts, "No, you missed," Christopher goes right along with him. It's hard to think of any other game that generates such absolute trust among its players.

Trust is just one of the values of the game. Another is justice, which is dispensed with such high standards that the Supreme Court itself might find it hard to keep pace. Watch when the two sides for playing guns are being picked. If one side gets "stuck" with the littlest player, compensation will be awarded by giving that side one of the new "mod squad" machine guns; or if one side ends up with the big kids, that side will agree to use sticks as guns, while the side with the younger kids is assigned the good guns. By the way, playing guns is the only form of play that brings kids of all ages together. Guns are the great equalizer.

In addition, this game draws a clear line between good and bad. Morality is made explicit: there are good guys and bad guys, but no neutrals.

On top of all this, we have yet to consider how playing guns stimulates the child's dream world. With these toys and pretend weapons, youngsters can make believe they are living in any century, in any place, playing all kinds of roles: knights, pirates, cowboys, soldiers, cops, and spacemen.

As your dreamer plays guns, keep track of what roles he plays. Does his play tend more toward future themes, like space, or past ones, like cowboys? Does playing guns involve children of different ages? Can you describe the instances of trust and justice in your child's play?

DIARY:

4

Jump Rope

OBJECTIVE:
OBSERVING AND
FOSTERING LANGUAGE
DEVELOPMENT

Last Easter our neighbor had a little French girl visiting for the holidays. The fact that the mademoiselle didn't speak a dime's worth of English did not stop her and Erin from becoming bosom buddies. What brought them together? Jump rope.

Jump rope is an international favorite that knows no boundaries. Everybody has played by its rules and sung its jingles: "Ibbity, bibbety, shibbity, sab." "Eeny, meeny, miney, mo." Who could listen to these chants and manage to keep their feet still? Hearing them, even the most nervous newcomer has to feel immediately at home.

But playing jump rope is more than a passport to friendship. Dreamers use it as a private means for expanding and refining their language by chanting or making up jumping jingles. Such tunes are often loaded with literary devices—alliterations, onomatopoeia, and so forth. Erin created jumping lyrics that combine different months—for example, "Jumber," which is a mix of June and September. On other occasions, she added an extra syllable to "Twin Towers," making it "Twin-ton Towers." This helped keep the beat she needed in a jumping jingle.

Don't be fooled into thinking that making up jumping jingles is a bunch of nonsense or a silly waste of time. At its very best, it represents the child's efforts to explore and stretch the creative limits of her native tongue. Since jumping rope can be done in private, it fits in nicely with the dreamer's style. In only a few other situations will you find the mind as relaxed and open to experiment with language as when the youngster is playing jump rope: it not only jolts the body but also jogs the mind into playful and imaginative moods.

Here is an activity that will help expand such moods: While your child is jumping, call out a word or event and see if she can come up with a new word for it. Erin thought of "bap" to describe a baby's burp and "plume," which is a hybrid of "plum" and "prune."

DIARY:

5

Fun
Fighting

OBJECTIVE:
DEMONSTRATING SIGNS
OF LOVE AND AFFECTION

"He's dead! He's dead!" shrieked Erin. "I knocked daddy out cold!"

I wasn't really out, just pooped and playing possum after having survived three rounds of what most kids swear is the greatest fun in the world—"play fighting with Daddy." Even though I played dead, I knew the jig was up as soon as Erin pried open my eyelids and yelled, "He's still in there—CHARGE!"

Once again, I was fair game and my three kids pounced on me as they would a trampoline. But I turned the tables and went after them, managing to snare Erin who was to become a victim of the dirtiest trick in fun fighting—tickling.

Such roughhousing activities are great for the dreamer. After spending so much time absorbed in her private thoughts, tickling and general roughhousing are a great release. In a sense they clear the air and allow the dreamer to return to her private world with her head in much better working order.

There's another bonus to roughhousing, and that is its emotional payoff. Rough physical play is one of the few ways in which the dreamer can directly express her feelings. Remember that she is a shut-in, trapped in her dream world. Yet, like all of us, she wants to keep in touch and to know that she is still loved and wanted. Fun fighting provides this assurance. It has the same effect as the rocking and hugging and other physical signs of love that she received as a tiny baby.

Unfortunately as kids grow older, we stop showing our love through physical touch and expect our words to do the trick. But they are a poor substitution, especially for the dreamer. Consequently, the dreamer often looks for physical signs of affection through rough-and-tumble play with chums.

True, it is sometimes hard to tell the difference between such good-natured horseplay and really mean fighting. Here are some clues to help you identify fun fighting:

> *Chasing:* This is a main feature of fun fighting. Others include running, tumbling, rolling, and jumping.
>
> *Punching:* The fist is the key. In fun fighting, it is only slightly cupped or else is completely open as it would be in delivering a slap.
>
> *Screaming:* The eyes bulge, and the mouth is wide open, emitting squealing, laughing, and screaming sounds.

Does your child's "horsing around" always involve all these three key behaviors? Or does she stress only one of them? Does your child roughhouse with certain playmates more than with others?

DIARY:

6

TV:
The Dream Machine

OBJECTIVE:
MEETING THE DREAMER'S
NEED FOR ACHIEVEMENT

What do Sigmund Freud, Benjamin Spock, and Bugs Bunny have in common? In different ways, they have all shed some light on what makes your children tick. In fact, Bugs and his creators, like the writers of Saturday morning TV shows, may keep closer tabs on the pulse and tastes of our young than anyone has ever given them credit for.

This observation may be hard to accept, but the proof is all around us. Compare the top ten "educational" hits of the season with "The Fonz," "Hulk," or "Batman" and you will find that there is not even a contest. But why? It is not just a matter of educational shows versus fun ones. There's more to it than that. My hunch is that those shows that keep in better touch with our psychological needs are the ones that win the rating wars.

Take "Star Trek" as an example. Year after year, its followers, the "Trekkies," who range in age from six to ninety-six, continue to add to their ranks. Distributors claim that the program is shown in so many countries that the sun never sets on the show's crew.

To have such an attraction, the show obviously has to be doing something right. In this case the producers have touched a sensitive psychological nerve that's alive in all of us: the need to achieve. We all have a need to "make it." Kids in particular are unsure whether they can cut the mustard in the outside world. There, beyond the circle of one's family, one can no longer take certain things for granted. Love, recognition, acceptance—all have to be won; nothing is free. The outside world is totally alien territory, but it is not too unlike those worlds visited by the *Enterprise*, the space ship skippered by Captain Kirk. On board, the crew acts like a family, while the ship itself serves as a halfway house: it allows our heroes to experience extraterrestrial adventures and yet remain tied securely to their family. In short, the *Enterprise* is a psychological vehicle that can be used to test the outside world without getting hurt.

Of the crew, there are none better at showing youngsters how to meet the test of the outside world than Mr. Spock and Captain Kirk. Spock is the mastermind and true-blue, ever-reliable buddy. Captain Kirk, a father figure, is quick, dedicated, and always ready to pull you out of any scrape or push you to new heights. Other than Bones, the doctor who's the softy on the show, the rest of the crew play bit parts. Interestingly, they are all men. Without a mixed cast, there are no specified girl or boy behaviors. This takes the pressure off the young viewer to conform to strict sex-role identity

("Only boys do that"; "How unlady like"). In addition, all the crew are approximately the same age, which frees the child from having to meet age expectations ("A five-year-old" child never does that").

For the child who is branching out on his own, whether by starting nursery school or making new friends, programs like "Star Trek" offer a dream world where he can find respite from a lot of the sticky problems that accompany his moves toward independence. On such programs the good guy with whom the viewer identifies always wins or achieves his goal. The good guy's success motivates the youngster to take on the "Star Trek" roles in his play, during which he encounters and copes with some real problems. Eventually, what has been learned in play is transferred to the child's everyday behavior. Without the safe and secure dream world of TV where the good guy always wins, the child might not engage in achievement-oriented or competitive types of play. Such play leads to the development of real strategies for achievement in the outside world.

Certain types of TV programs seem well suited for meeting achievement needs. They usually have the following characteristics:

1. A magician or mastermind who can be depended upon in a pinch.
2. A club, gang, or crew who take the place of the family (they usually have a hideout, spaceship, or some kind of halfway house).
3. Masked animals or strange looking characters who reveal neither sex nor age, which relieves the child from the pressure of having to measure up to age and sex expectations.

If your youngster is about to get his first taste of the real world outside his home, it would be a good idea to steer him toward this type of television show.

Of the characteristics mentioned above, which best typifies your child's favorite TV program? Which characteristic appears to inspire the most fantasy in your child's play? Do your child's best friends enjoy the same programs he does?

7

The Funny Papers

OBJECTIVE:
OBSERVING HOW THE DREAMER LEARNS ABOUT OUR WORLD VIA COMICS

The best sleeping pill ever invented for children outside of PBS television is a discussion of current events at the dinner table. Nothing else works as fast at sedating a youngster as today's news.

All kidding aside, however, children should be aware of the things going on around them. Besides the facts acquired, such an awareness has to broaden their outlook, which is usually narrow, if not self-centered.

Nonetheless, for my kids the evening papers were good for only one thing: "Snoopy." Leafing through the *Tribune* on her way to the funnies one night, Erin ran across an editorial on evolution that had a cartoon showing an ape with a man's head. She cracked up: "Look at the gorilla with the man's face."

I decided it wouldn't hurt in passing to take a stab at explaining the theory to her: "Scientists think that a very long time ago we all came from monkeys." Before I could continue she unloaded ten questions on me: "Was Gramps a monkey? Will the monkeys in the zoo turn to people? Who changes the monkeys? Do we turn back into monkeys when we die?"

As I fielded her questions, you could see this theory beginning to jell in her mind. You wouldn't believe this was the same little girl who the day before had walked away from a TV special about a space shot. Today I couldn't feed her information fast enough. She'd take any science I had.

What triggered this turnaround? What was so special about the cartoon? Quite simply, the ape-man was a riddle and no child likes to be stumped, especially a dreamer who's in her public cycle, seeking information. In fact, puzzles and riddles often trip the spring that sends the dreamer into this cycle. While in the public cycle, the dreamer is not only open to information, but also drops her guard to the point where she might even express some deep feelings. And cartoons are a good way of helping youngsters get such things off their chests. That is precisely what Erin did with her bossy piano teacher: after we had discussed a cartoon of a Latin American politician in the hip pocket of a general, Erin went on to draw one of herself in the hip pocket of her piano teacher. The piano teacher never caught on, but Erin knew exactly what she was doing.

To see how your child reacts to cartoons, collect some from various magazines and newspapers. Once you start to show them to children on a regular basis, it doesn't take very long before the children become enthusiasts of editorial art. Pieces of art that really open up the dreamer, inspiring her to express her feelings as well as to seek information, have these features:

1. Animal characters.
2. Running, chasing, or acting scenes.
3. Exaggerations (a foot-long rose).
4. Puzzles or paradoxes (commuters rowing a bus as a result of the gasoline shortage). Cartoons that contain puzzles or paradoxes are the most effective type.

At first, just show the cartoons and make passing comments only. When the child asks something about the cartoon, you can respond in more depth. As the child becomes familiar with this medium, she'll start providing her own interpretations. Finally, you may be able to get her to express her feelings through her own drawings. This is very likely to happen because cartoons are geared toward putting the dreamer in her public cycle.

DIARY:

8

Bullies

OBJECTIVE:
RECOGNIZING HOW IMAGINATION
DEFUSES AGGRESSIVE BEHAVIOR

There's one on every block. He may live only a few doors away. In Erin's case, he even went to the same nursery school. His name was Frank the Tank: a pint-sized Attila the Hun whose bullying on the playgrounds knew no bounds.

His assaults were legendary and his victims numerous. Of all his targets, Frank's favorites were unsuspecting kids on a seesaw. Frank would forcibly seize the seesaw and turn it into a catapult, snapping its occupants far off into space like human cannonballs. Next Frank would unleash his fury on the school slide. As he lumbered up its ladder, fellow climbers bailed out of his way, giving him an open route to the top where he played king of the mountain, defying anyone to use the slide. If there were no takers, he and his henchmen, a spineless lot of kids, would rumble over to the swings where they tied the chains in knots. Finally, Frank would draw a bead on the kickball games and snatch as many of the balls as his stubby little arms could hold. Then, when ordered by the teacher on school yard duty to return the balls to their rightful owners, the Tank would fire the balls at his classmates as if they were bowling pins waiting to be mowed down.

Without doubt, Frank was on his way to the FBI's Ten Most Wanted list. It was only a matter of time. Regardless of the measures taken, nothing could curb his temper. So you can imagine how uneasy we felt with the class picnic coming up. It was the last event of the school year, and there was no way that Frank was going to miss it.

The picnic site was on the edge of a large farm dotted with orchards, streams, boulders, open fields, and clumps of thick, wild berry bushes.

It didn't take Frank long to start his shenanigans. But since there were no swings or slides to ravage, he was at a temporary loss, during which a string of marvelous events unfolded. First Erin stumbled across a long, narrow branch, perfect for a sword or spear. Within seconds of her discovery came word of another. Matt Hopper, while wading through the stream, had found a handful of beautiful green pebbles. In a flash, the discoverers were surrounded by an army of playmates chanting, "It's a buried treasure!" "Let's play pirates." "Erin's captain, she has the sword." "The big rock is our ship; where's yours?" Everyone was chipping in his own little dream. The result was a huge adventure fantasy that swept away all the youngsters for the whole afternoon—that is, all of them but the Tank, who had been totally shut out. Even his henchmen had left him flat. In a last ditch effort to rally his forces, Frank charged toward the pirates like a killer whale. The kids scattered into the bushes and between the rocks. Poor Frank, being a whale in both size and agility, was far too clumsy to catch any of his intended victims. Crestfallen, the Tank broke down and by the time the school bus rolled up to take everyone home, even Frank could be found following Erin and Matthew in search of the elusive hidden treasure.

The play fantasy, which required a keen mind rather than the brute strength of the bully, was apparently the cause of Frank's nose dive. Once children rely on cunning and imagination rather than raw force, play becomes less suited to the power-hungry bully and more geared to the creative tendencies of young children.

One activity we've found that really fires the imagination of the dreamer is playing "Robinson Crusoe." Tell the child she's been shipwrecked and has only the following supplies: tree bark, branches, stones, sand, some string, a spoon, and a pail of water. How would she survive? What would she do? Using the spoon, Erin once dug up an old turkey carcass and, after washing it, made its hollow bones into a flute with which to attract passing ships. Next, she used the turkey's breast and rib cage as a mask to scare off the island's cannibals.

How many of these different objects can your child imaginatively transform? Does she use her supplies as tools, as Erin did in digging with the spoon? Or do the supplies become ends in themselves? On one occasion Erin used the spoon as a microphone and the string as its antenna. Does you child, like Erin, use the objects in combination, or does she use them separately?

DIARY: _____

9

TV, Toys, and Creative Play

OBJECTIVE: TAPPING THE CREATIVE POTENTIAL OF ANY TV SHOW

If you asked Erik to rank the most important people in the world, they would be Santa, Ronald McDonald, and the Lone Ranger. In a showdown vote, the masked man would win hands down. Our little guy was so into westerns that once when the TV conked out in the middle of a saloon shoot-out, he yelled at me, "Clean out the dead cowboys from the bottom of the set. It'll work then!" Impatient with my fumblings to revive the set, he buckled on his six-gun and galloped off to continue the shoot-out on his own.

As powerful as TV is, there is not always a direct link between the child's play and what he just viewed on the TV screen. The linkage depends on the presence of an essential ingredient: the props. Without the guns, hats, holsters, boots, and chaps, the youngster doesn't have any real chance of making the masked man come alive. In short, props fuel the child's dreams, and they don't have to be brightly gleaming new toys to do this. Sticks, towels, and old hats will work nicely.

Because they meet a psychological need, adventure shows with cops or cowboys require only the slim support of props or toys. In contrast, educational programs need the full support of the parent. In other words, "Sesame Street" will have a payoff only if you spend time hammering home the show's message.

Let's be honest; you know what kids will watch when you're not around. "Mr. Rogers" is bound to run a poor second to "Superman" every time. But this isn't a total loss. The right props can trigger some very creative play during this stage of life. If you're not available to turn your child's TV watching into a learning experience, you can try to make it a creative one with the right toys. Here are some of the earmarks of creative play:

1. Creative play lasts a long time.
2. Like a soap opera, it has many subplots.
3. Many of these plots are just copies of TV fare, but the child may create new, original characters for the story.
4. Often the play is solitary, the child off in a dream world by himself.
5. If interrupted, the creative spell is broken. Unlike a ball game with clear-cut rules for starting and stopping the event, creative play, once stopped, cannot continue.

Most of the points mentioned should show up in the dreamer's play if the props are matched thematically to the shows that the child views.

10

Painting

OBJECTIVE:
IDENTIFYING THE STAGES OF
PAINTING THROUGH WHICH
THE CREATIVE CHILD PASSES

While we were walking to his kindergarten one morning, Christopher told me of his latest art project—a painting of the first man. Expecting to view a portrait that in some remote way resembled Adam, I was floored to see his picture of a military figure standing in a boat and pointing. "Isn't that George Washington?" I asked. "Right," he answered. "What about Adam," I insisted, "wasn't he the first man?" "Nah," Chris shrugged, "only if you count foreigners." At first I was so taken aback by his cockeyed view of history that I didn't notice the change in his artistic style. Up to this point his paintings had looked like nothing but explosive nervous energy. Now they smacked of realism (the George Washington figure), signaling a leap from the poetic to the inventive stage. Painting is a creative expression that the child experiences differently in each of the three stages.

STEP 1: DREAMER

The child's head is swimming with images, but before he can paint anything, the dreamer must get a feel for the materials he'll be using. So the bulk of his time is spent eating, sniffing, or smearing paint all over himself, as well as everything within reach—tables, curtains, walls, and rugs. Once he has established familiarity with his materials, the dreamer is ready to commit his impressions to paper. His first impressions usually come out looking like bull's-eyes whose rings are painted in contrasting colors. Often the paint from one ring either drips or runs into another ring. Next come self-portraits, which are just as sloppy as the bull's eyes. In fact, some of these can turn your stomach. They look like omelets or melted plastic faces with globs instead of eyes or mouths.

Clearly the dreamer has merely been acquiring his artistic legs. Though shaky and unsteady, he's finally ready to take the next step in artistic development.

STEP 2: POET

What happens during this period is a real shot in the arm for the young artist. In addition to believing that he can paint anything, he is convinced that his works can come alive. Although much of the poet's painting is purely abstract, it is meant to tell a real story. As far as that goes, the poet-artist is of the opinion that all pictures are real and breathing. He sees little difference between your ID photo and the actual flesh-and-blood you standing in front of him. Why else would Christopher, on coming across an illustration of Peter Rabbit pinned under a fence, try to lift the fence to free his hero?

Don't jump on the poet for his views. Pretty soon nature will have run its course, and such beliefs will start to fade. The first hint of change comes when the youngster begins to tear up his work. Realizing his pictures stink and in no way measure up to the models he's trying to copy, it dawns on the young artist that his painting, which looks so different from the real object, can't be real itself. This is a crushing realization.

STEP 3: INVENTOR

This blow to his creative ego carries over to the inventor stage and sends the young artist running scared and searching for a new and safer style. Basically, the inventor becomes a stickler for detail as he attempts to paint pictures that are carbon copies of real things. Take a good look at the inventor's brush strokes. They're short and choppy as if they had been programmed by a computer. That is the inventor's way of reducing mistakes, but it also acts to curb his wild imagination. Trial-and-error learning and mistakes are at the heart of creativity but, for the moment, this type of risk taking has been lost.

Soon the inventor begins to take risks again. Gradually he gives the figures he draws their own hairstyles and clothes. With this, he is individualizing and making his paintings personal and unique, rather than sticking safely to faithful copies. Next the young artist goes even further out on a limb and starts installing special features on his figures—big ears, muscles, fat bellies, and so forth. Finally, one day when you least expect it, he paints feelings on the faces of his characters. The conservatism of the early part of this period has now been broken.

To see if your child has freed himself of this conservative bind, ask him to paint a picture of an ugly and a beautiful person. How does the inventor paint these two types? Does he stress only hairstyles and clothing, or does he use various body parts? If the artist has really progressed, he'll rely more on expressions or feelings to convey the differences between the two figures. His painting may show an understanding that beauty is only skin deep, that what makes a person pretty or attractive is not so much his outside looks as what's going on inside of him. The artist may reveal this understanding by using facial expressions, such as smiles or frowns, in his artwork.

DIARY:

11

Nightmare
at the
Opera

OBJECTIVE:
RECOGNIZING HOW MUSIC AFFECTS
THE EMOTIONAL DEVELOPMENT
OF THE DREAMER

To plug a little more cultural zip into Christopher's otherwise lowbrow musical diet of "The Muffin Man" and "Twinkle, Twinkle . . . ," we dragged him to the opera. Once the curtain went up, his eyes fell on the wiry, spry conductor and the whalelike diva. As the maestro flailed his baton, the diva's voice grew louder and louder until finally our boy screeched, "STOP that guy from beating the fat lady with his stick!" "Sh-sh," I hushed, "he's not." "Then why," asked Christopher, "is she screaming?"

The first round in Christopher's musical development obviously went to him. So did the second: he now used music not to any creative end but as an outlet for the frequent jealousy he felt toward his new baby brother. At one point, Christopher came up with this ditty, "Erik, Erik, Mom's baby. Erik, Erik, Mom's boy. Twist his neck, hit him on the head. Throw him in a ditch and he'll be dead!" Even after he outgrew this sense of rivalry, Christopher still used music as an emotional crutch to help him out of tight squeezes. During his first extended time away from home at nursery school, he constantly hummed "Rock-a-Bye Baby," nursery rhymes, and other little songs. They were his security blanket, a way of keeping alive some memories of the warmth and friendliness of home while physically separated from it. One of his more alert nursery school teachers used Christopher's preoccupation with singing to sharpen some basic mental skills: the groundwork for counting was laid by having him beat rhythm sticks to different records, while his first notion of the spatial concept of up and down came from singing the scale.

However, for Christopher, the best thing about music was its power to put him in the mood to fantasize. To inspire such a mood in your child, get a jazz and a classical record; the former is rhythmic and melodic, while the latter is harmonic and dissonant. Each type of record will trigger different forms of fantasizing. When you play each record, ask the youngster to pretend that he is the wind getting up in the morning; a rain shower on a very hot day; a forest fire; or the ground during an earthquake. As he's playing out these themes, note the form of fantasy that he uses—movement or dance, acting or dramatic expressions, or singing or talking. The more these three forms are combined, the deeper the child's fantasy and the better able he is to express his inner creative stirrings.

12

The
Class
Clown

OBJECTIVE:
USING PUPPETS TO
STIR THE DREAMER'S
IMAGINATION

Who doesn't remember the class clown? My earliest recollection puts him somewhere in the second grade, but surely not in nursery school. Yet in no uncertain terms, this was the picture I was getting from Erik's nursery school teacher: "He's always fooling and horsing around. Nothing mean, mind you. But those silly faces he makes crack everyone up and completely disrupt our snack time."

What fuels these antics? There are bookshelves packed with theories. But in Erik's case it all boiled down to one thing: his hair. It was like one huge Brillo pad. He was a regular Harpo Marx and, as such, suffered the brunt of many of his classmates' jokes. Anything that makes a dreamer stand out is a sore spot. Dreamers want to get along with everyone and be in control of their own lives. At this point, Erik was losing that control because of the needling he was getting from chums; so he turned the tables and controlled the situation by becoming a clown. His classmates now laughed with him, not at him.

As a clown, Erik was always on his toes: fast, quick-witted, and spontaneous. However, the problem was how to channel these fast-flowing creative juices into more constructive, if not socially acceptable, behaviors. What made this more of a problem was that because Erik was a dreamer, any tampering with his feelings resulted in his pulling back, closing up, and becoming ice cold toward you. At least with clowning, he was openly trying to cope with his problems. There were a number of ways to try to channel his creativity into more acceptable behavior. We tried doll play, but that proved to be only an escape route to his private world. During such play, most of his action-oriented ideas quickly dried up. However, the dolls did trigger another option: puppets. They indeed did work by capturing the spunk and spirit of clowning, while offering the dreamer the privacy to hide behind the personality of the puppet.

Interestingly, not all puppets worked. Only the sock variety brought out the full range of the dreamer's emotions. With this variety, the puppet's facial expressions can be easily changed from wild smiles to bent frowns. But the socks enabled Erik to do more than just verbalize his feelings; with them he could act out his feelings. He could form a fist with the sock puppet and throw a punch to show anger; make a handshake to show friendship; have a fist hitting an open palm to depict frustration or impatience; wipe away a tear to show forgiveness. Erik demonstrated affection by using one sock puppet to stroke the top of the other. On another occasion, he provided physical care by rubbing his two sock puppets together, trying to warm the one that had been left out in the cold.

Provide your dreamer with a set of sock puppets, one for each hand. They're easy to make. You may want to draw on them or attach some buttons for facial features. What feelings does the child act out? Do they deal with physical needs, like feeding, or more social needs like two friends holding hands? How do the puppets handle fear?

DIARY:

13

Drawing

OBJECTIVE:
RECOGNIZING THE STAGES
OF DRAWING THAT THE
DREAMER EXPERIENCES

In my line of work as a professor, it's easy to get a swelled head, especially if you're still wet behind the ears and on your first teaching job. Luckily I met Jessie, a scrappy, no-nonsense four-year-old who put me in my place before I could do any real damage.

Jessie's mother, a student of mine, was planning to go back to school full time but was worried about how her little girl would react to baby-sitters and other new adjustments, such as day care. Of course she consulted the right person. I could psych out Jessie in a wink simply by running my expertly trained eyes through a batch of the child's drawings.

Once I caught a glimpse of Jessie's picture of her father I had her pegged. She had him looking like a bald banana with a stick body. To me, the signs were quite clear: Jessie was intellectually slow, socially backward, and most likely an emotionally dependent clinging vine. Then I bumped into Jessie's father one day after class—a nice fellow, though bald as an eagle and with a beak to match. Obviously Jessie was as sound as a bell. She had ingeniously drawn a banana figure to capture her father's two most prominent features: a large nose and a smooth head.

I was the banana. Such quick diagnoses based on tests without observations of the child's play aren't worth the paper they're written on. That goes for all tests from an IQ to the draw-a-man variety I was using. Jessie's play would have shown that she was operating in the dreamer stage. As a dreamer, much of her play would have been a series of one large exaggeration after another. Dreamers love to blow things out of proportion. In this case, Jessie used the symbol of a banana to exaggerate her father's features.

There are two other characteristics of drawing during the dreaming phase that are worth noting:

1. The dreamer loves to scribble and doodle on anything from paper to walls to tables to mirrors, which means *never* leave lipstick hanging around. If anything, this is a time for water colors or water-based magic markers unless you want a house with a permanent coat of graffiti.

2. Another feature of the dreamer's drawings is the parts that are missing. Legs, arms, heads, and feet are always unconnected and left dangling in mid-air. The dreamer makes the connections in her mind but not on paper.

To get an idea of how the dreamer uses paints and colors to dress up her drawings, look over activity 10 in this chapter.

If from your experiences you've judged your child to be a dreamer, here are some concrete points to look for in her drawing:

1. Stick figures.
2. Body parts exaggerated and unconnected or floating in space.
3. Comments always accompanying the drawing to tie together the floating body parts.
4. General absence of clothing.

Have your youngster draw some family members. Do these portraits correspond to the above points?

DIARY:

14

Blocks

OBJECTIVE:
USING BLOCKS
TO EXPRESS POWER

One thing you could count on with Erin was that you could never count on her. She was the pokiest kid on two feet, always in a fog and lost in one of her daydreams. There was the time she left to wash her hands for dinner and forgot to come back to eat. Her excuse was, "I guess I overwashed." On checking the bathroom, I found that it certainly did look as if she had overwashed, for sitting in the sink was nearly a year's supply of soap bars, all caked together to form one giant igloo.

Soap bars and, for that matter, any building materials that resemble blocks or scraps of wood are ideal for the dreamer because, unlike drawing or painting, blocks permit the dreamer to put ideas into action rather than simply commiting them to paper.

However, not all block play serves as a testing ground for new ideas. At times, it acts as a convenient vehicle for experiencing power, as when the youngster levels one of her own masterpieces. That is a dreamer's way of doing something wrong without getting punched. There are other occasions when this destruction is really just a way of getting back at you. If the dreamer feels you've been unfair, she'll build something you like and then destroy the project in front of your very eyes. Or she can be more subtle. Once after Erin was banished to her room for some misdeed, she kept building skyscrapers and kicking them over; this doesn't mean much unless you realize that I work in a very tall building.

Admittedly not all demolitions stem from the reasons just mentioned. Some are triggered by fights over how to use the blocks. Space and materials are limited: it's either going to be Erin's tower or Erik's airport, not both. In most cases, nothing ever gets built. With all kids, and ours were no exception, most cooperative block play at best leads only to one builder's copying the efforts of the other. On the other hand, most creative building happens when the dreamer is alone and using small "LEGO®" type of blocks. Such blocks are so intricate that they corner all the youngster's attention, leaving little room for dealing with anything else.

Under what conditions does your child's block play seem to thrive? When working alone or with others? When using big or small blocks? Here is a guide for rating the developmental level of your youngster's creative block play:

1. Initially the dreamer makes only horizontal structures, using one or two blocks. It's as if she were building a ranch house.
2. Next the dreamer builds forts, using front and side walls.
3. Towers represent a more advanced level.
4. Finally the dreamer creates whole cities that are interconnected with bridges, ramps, highways, and tunnels. During this phase, the dreamer personalizes her efforts by pinning labels on the structures: "There's where Mommy works." "See Nana's house."

15

Water
Play

OBJECTIVE:
USING WATER
TO STIMULATE THE
DREAMER'S CREATIVITY

For Christopher's birthday we planned an elaborate celebration: a trip to Asbury Amusement Park on the New Jersey shore, with a beach party thrown in. Yet as soon as he got wind of the plan, Christopher crumpled to the floor and bawled, "I ain't going to no beach!" "But you loved the ocean last year," I countered. "Yeah, but not when it flushed."

Come to think of it, the pounding surf can be pretty scary even for a grown-up, let alone for a little guy like Chris. Poor kid, you can easily imagine the tug of war pulling inside of him: "How can I go to the beach I love and be near the waves I hate?" The beach finally won out.

It amazes me how children, despite all kinds of fears, take to water like fish. There has to be some natural attraction. One such draw is that water has a "mothering effect"; it soothes and lulls. It is a paradise for dreamers where they can lose themselves in one thought after another. A warm bath works the same magic on kids; it tranquilizes or "dreamatizes" them. Washing kids while they are in the tub shatters this peace of mind and will evoke mighty roars of protest.

I just let the child soak. (*But never leave a child alone, even for a second:* Bathtub drownings are one of the leading causes of children's deaths.) If the dirt doesn't melt away after a good soaking, then work up a big head of lather on your soap and use it to scrub off the grime while you towel down the youngster. Generally children don't fight too much against the rubbing and scrubbing that goes along with being dried off. It's while they're in the tub and off in dreamland that you have to play along with them.

For an activity that caters to the dreamer's wild imagination, add some food coloring to bath water. Aside from coloring the water, it will color the child's mood as well: red for passion; yellow for happiness; green for hope; purple for anger, and so on. Also make sure that the dreamer has a variety of toys: some that sink, others that float, and a few sponges as well. Next, supply him with a number of plastic containers and spoons that hold different amounts of water. A handful of little soldiers or wooden figures will complete the list of water toys for the dreamer. The more water toys the dreamer simultaneously plays with, the faster his imagination works. Having no shape itself, water offers no barrier to the dreamer's imagination.

What are your child's favorite water toys? What colors does he like best? What toys does he play with most? Are there days when he prefers the soldiers over the floating toys?

DIARY:

16

Feelings Through Movement

OBJECTIVE:
USING BODY LANGUAGE
CREATIVELY

Erin's two greatest loves in life were cats and telephones. Unfortunately, as things sometimes go with little kids, she wasn't making too much headway with either. Finally, life reached a breaking point. Smokey Joe, our Angora cat, all but ignored her, and she got nothing but busy signals everytime she dialed the telephone. In a fit of desperation, she yelled at Smokey Joe, who did nothing except purr. "See," she screamed, "even Smokey doesn't want me. Hear his busy signal?"

It wasn't too long after this outburst that her luck began to change. Later in the day while I was in the tub, the phone rang and Erin answered it. The caller insisted Erin take down his name and started to spell it out, "B-r-o-w..." Before he could finish, she broke in, gulped, and doodling in the air, asked, "How do you make a *B*? Does it go this way or that way?"

Erin blew her big chance. Brown hung up in frustration. But just as hung up was Erin, *her* problem being written language. When under such pressure as talking on the phone, inventors fall back to earlier forms of communications, namely, body language, a combination of hand signals mixed with grimaces. Though regular speech eventually takes over, body movements like Erin's doodling in the air continue to play an important part in our lives. They help express feelings that can't be put into words. Obviously Erin was upset over not being able to take Brown's message and so turned to doodling. It served as an outlet for her disappointment and frustrations. Dancers do the same thing. They use body movements to express feelings.

Pantomiming is a good activity for helping inventors express feelings that are otherwise hard to get out. Have your youngster mime the following: feeling hurt, tired, happy, lonely, excited, and surprised.

DIARY:

17

Hell
on Wheels

OBJECTIVE:
USING IMAGINATION
TO QUELL A DISRUPTIVE DREAMER

A humorist wise in the ways of the world once quipped that there are two ways to travel: first class or with children. Anyone who's ever taken a trip with my kids would add a third option: without them.

Though we tried to cut out most family trips, once a year we all found ourselves stuffed into the same little car for a two-day jaunt en route to our summer vacation. Believe me, a couple of days on the road with my gang and a year's rest wouldn't be enough to straighten out your nerves. For openers, one could always count on Christopher vomiting in the back seat and Erin's pleading for us to turn back home and get the teddy bear she'd left on the porch. Naturally these trips brought out the best in me. I never failed to plan our trip for the day on which all existing heat records were to be broken. But Erik's timing was even better. Like clockwork, he always had to "pee" as soon as we pulled out of a gas station.

Until now I've only touched on the good points of the trip and have not dared to mention the thing that really made our blood boil: the incessant teasing, fighting, and nagging upon which three bored kids, packed in a car like sardines, thrive.

Car trips are an emotional pressure cooker. If you can imagine what it would be like to be cooped up for months on a submarine, then you can understand what it is like for young children hemmed into the back seat of a car. They're starved for stimulation, and, with the slightest provocation, all hell will break loose.

How does one deal with such a situation? There are two ways: One involves spotting the danger signals that lead to trouble, and the other has to do with a special toy.

1. *DANGER SIGNALS*: There are four conditions that lead children to become unruly: (1) if two kids are having fun playing together and a third butts in; (2) the presence of food, which is volatile and can be thrown, spilled, played with, or snatched from another; (3) drowsiness, or the need for sleep, which makes a child like a wounded animal, ill-tempered and mean, ripe for a fight; (4) boldness resulting from the child's feeling that he can get away with murder while on the road because you can't punish him as easily and effectively as you can at home.

These conditions are troublesome in all areas of the child's life. But when they occur in the tight space of a car or even on a trip in a school bus, they wreak havoc. This havoc can be lessened if one is alert to the conditions that set it off. However, there's another measure one can take: a toy that prevents these conditions from arising.

2. *TOY:* Pack a battery-powered tape recorder and a few blank cassettes and, presto, your offspring will switch from being provocateurs to TV producers, acting out commercials on tape, interviewing each other, singing until they're hoarse, or even cooking up slapstick routines, a la the Marx Brothers. In addition, bring along some tapes upon which you've recorded their favorite shows, nursery rhymes, or storybooks. Unlike books, which allow children to sit back and absorb stimulation, tape recorders allow youngsters to actively create their own entertainment.

The tapes obviously aren't going to save the whole trip. But they do keep kids out of your hair for long stretches of time during which you can relax and store up the stamina you're going to need when trouble calls.

Keep in mind that there are certain characteristics in stories that keep kids glued to their seats. So in preparing your tapes, be sure that they include action, movement, and conflict.

DIARY:

18

Temper Tantrums

OBJECTIVE: CONTROLLING TEMPER TANTRUMS

When pressure builds, little children have a number of ways of letting off steam. However, for the dreamer who can't express himself or who has parents who aren't attuned to his needs, there is only one outlet: the temper tantrum.

Fortunately, like a simmering volcano ready to skyrocket, tantrums give off danger signals before they blow. The initial stage of the tantrum is generally called "brooding" and is signaled by the child's being picky at dinner, grouchy with grown-ups, and unable to sleep or to mix well with friends at school or at home. Brooding soon builds up to the first recognizable signs of the tantrum: crying and screaming. Next there are bouts of biting, kicking, and throwing oneself to the ground. Then there's the grand finale, the "blue-out"—that is, turning blue and rigid while holding one's breath.

Brooding usually stems from some legitimate frustration and leads to crying when we are not responsive to the dreamer's needs. When kicking and biting occur, we've gone too far or mistaken the problem and given it the wrong remedy. In desperation the youngster turns to the "blue-out," which really brings you to your knees, both literally and figuratively. The blue-out is dangerous: a red flag that your relationship with your child has really gone downhill.

If not checked at this point, the child will continue to use the tantrum as a way of dodging responsibilities or of getting his own way. When used as a dodge, the tantrum is no longer a legitimate outlet for frustration; the child is using it to control you. If the tantrums constantly occur in public places, such as shopping malls, you may be fairly sure you are being manipulated. The child is trying to embarrass you. If she succeeds and you give in or blow up, you may be establishing a pattern that's hard to break. In such a situation, you may want to walk away until you have cooled off. Ignoring the tantrum may in itself be enough to squelch it. With older children, the tantrum takes the form of stubbornness. Instead of using physical force, the child at this age pits her will against yours.

No matter what form the tantrum takes, it's still triggered by the same basic cause: a feeling of being *cheated*. If the youngster senses he's being treated unfairly or cheated by you or others whom he really trusts, he then begins to feel that he is at the end of his rope and has no recourse other than throwing a tantrum.

The trick to handling tantrums is to nip them in the bud by pinpointing their causes. Most seem to start from one or a combination of the following conditions:

1. A broken promise.
2. A sudden order to a child who is engrossed in play to stop and come home for lunch or get ready for a nap.
3. The child's feeling that the parent is playing favorites.
4. Such stress to live up to adult standards that children who fail to meet the adult standards snap and go to pieces.
5. Parents who are themselves high strung and touchy under pressure.

Which of these conditions affect your dreamer?

The following are some preventive actions for dealing with each of the steps of a temper tantrum. Which work best with your dreamer?

Phases	Actions
BROODING	Depending on the child, you have three moves: (1) Directly ask what's bothering him. (2) Give an example: Are you mad because I didn't take you to the zoo as I promised? (3) Make up a story using one or more of the conditions that lead to a temper tantrum as your plot. Then ask how the child in the story felt and how you could help him feel better.
CRYING	At this point you have to act fast. For whatever reason, you weren't able to pinpoint the cause of his brooding so it's best to do something tangible for the youngster. Treat him in a special way. Do an extra favor for him, anything to demonstrate that you're trying to meet his needs.
KICKING	At this point you simply want to get the youngster's attention so you can try to help her again. Attention can be gained by scolding, physically restraining, walking away, or, as one ingenious father learned, by lying down on the ground and imitating the child's tantrum.
BLUE-OUT	Words won't do any longer. The child needs physical signs of security, warmth, and caring. Hold the youngster tenderly while rocking, stroking, and humming to her.

DIARY:

19

Pinocchio and Pooh: Pillars of Morality

OBJECTIVE:
UNDERSTANDING
IMMANENT JUSTICE

Fairy tales are far from frivolous; if anything, they're spiked with moral lessons. Pinocchio, for example, cannot lie without being given away by his long nose, while Pooh, a well-meaning but dumb little bear, is always paying the price for his greed. In one scene, after gorging himself with all of Rabbit's honey, this silly overstuffed bear gets stuck trying to wedge himself out of Rabbit's door.

Interestingly, neither Pinocchio nor Pooh feels these penalties are unjust because both are operating on the level of *immanent justice*, which is the belief that punishment is directly tied to one's misdeeds. Falling off a tree that one had been forbidden to climb or burning one's finger while playing with matches are examples of immanent justice. Young children basically feel that laws of morality are just like the laws of nature: If you jump off a building, you're going to get hurt; if you do something bad like stealing an apple, a suitable punishment would be to choke half to death.

A child's view of immanent justice goes through four phases. To determine your child's view, ask him to explain why a robber who was trying to get away by running across a bridge slipped and fell into the river below. The child's answers should fall into one of four categories: (1) The robber fell in because he was bad. (2) The bridge loosened one of its boards so he'd fall in. (3) The police, God, or some other force made the bridge shake so the robber would fall off. (4) It was an old bridge and he fell through one of the rotting planks.

The purest form of immanent justice is found in the first explanation. If you're bad, you're supposed to fall in; it's the law. The second and third explanations show a little more maturity. In the second explanation, the bridge seems to come alive, and in the third, some special outside power intervenes to assure that justice prevails. It is at this point that kids strongly believe that superheroes and mythological figures will come to one's rescue. The last statement shows an attempt to explain the event logically.

DIARY:

20

The Bogeyman

OBJECTIVE:
DEALING
WITH ANXIETIES

Just as you think you've discovered what makes your children tick, inevitably you run smack into their magical world and get completely sidetracked. Such was my recent experience when I took Christopher along on a business trip, and we stayed in a large, luxurious downtown hotel. No sooner had I put Chris to bed, than he barreled out of his room yelling, "Daddy, Daddy, it's a bogeyman! He's after me!" After comforting and reassuring him that everything was all right, I marched him back to bed. However, during the next hour this cycle was repeated so many times that I finally got fed up and shouted, "Look, we're on the forty-second floor, the windows are sealed, and the door has locks, chains, and bolts. HOW CAN ANYBODY GET IN HERE?" In desperation I dove on the floor, squirmed under Christopher's bed, grappled for a moment, and then came up dragging an imaginary bogeyman. With the monster in hand, I raced to the bathroom and flushed it down the toilet. Nothing ever cleared up a nightmare so fast, and nothing ever set me so straight about how a young dreamer thinks.

Of course all those statistics about the forty-second floor, and so on, did nothing for him. Why should they have? Dreamers aren't rational; they're magical. As far as Christopher was concerned, there was a bogeyman in his room and I had disposed of him as I would a real prowler. Youngsters can't separate what they imagine from what's actually happening. When you put a child to bed in a strange, dark room, his imagination begins to play tricks on him. Every shadow and creak becomes some horrible creature.

At the root of Christopher's nightmare was a lack of stimulation. In a dark room there's nothing to do so the mind begins to create things to occupy itself. The eerier these creations, the more entertaining, until an invisible line is crossed and these fantasies are twisted into Frankensteins.

The child can't stop seeking stimulation; it's his nature. However, he can avoid dark places, cemeteries, castles, haunted houses, or any other situation that triggers nightmares. Eventually the child realizes that strange places cause him to worry. This realization represents a big step in his development. It means that he can now distinguish between two types of fears: (1) real dangers—that is, real people, places, and things that can hurt him; and (2) anxieties or worries fashioned in the mind that can be painful but in a different way. These two fears can feed each other. One evening Christopher heard on the news that a whole school bus filled with children had been kidnapped. This real tragedy must have played on his mind all night, for the following morning he refused to take his bus to school.

It seems that young children have a variety of psychological fears that cause anxiety. If any of these fears show up in your child and become hard to shake, here are a few strategies that might help: (1) Night-lights are effective at warding off nightmares. (2) For a child who has to sleep in a strange or "haunted" room, the practice of letting him race around the place and explore all its nooks and crannies seems to provide the assurance that he needs. (3) Finally, when a child appears anxious, you should supervise the TV that he watches. Fantasy programs starring superheroes are less likely to produce anxiety than are realistic ones, such as news shows. The child is at the age when the real events of the world can easily set off a chain reaction of monstrous worries.

DIARY:

21

Imaginary Friends

OBJECTIVE:
COPING
WITH EMOTIONS
THROUGH FANTASY

Make-believe friends are fun for kids, and since they'll eat whatever is on the table and can squeeze into any old space, they are rarely a headache. However, if a dreamer gets carried away and thinks these "friends" are real, as Erin did, then you're in for some rough times.

It all started when Erin began to pretend she was an imaginary dog called "Ruffy." We went along with this image as best we could, even buying Ruffy a Snoopy cereal bowl for her breakfast. But I drew the line one morning when I shuffled into the bathroom and found my daughter urinating with one leg up in the air like a dog. It goes without saying that Ruffy was toilet trained on the spot. Yet a certain amount of leeway and understanding is needed when kids get caught up in the world of imaginary friends. Such friends pop up in children's lives for a whole stack of reasons. A child who is feeling down in the dumps may create a "superstar" who has all the qualities the child would love to have. Imaginary friends may also be created out of loneliness or as scapegoats to be blamed when things go wrong. Some kids even invent a "slave" whom they can easily boss around. Such an invention may occur when a youngster is having trouble making friends.

The list of needs for having an imaginary friend could fill a book: guilt, rage, jealousy, fear, and so forth. Though one can never be sure why the friend was created, it's a sure bet that there is some psychological reason for it.

To break through the veil of secrecy and gain some idea of your child's emotional needs, try the following: Tell her you used to have an imaginary pal when you were a kid. Make the friend a superstar and tell the child all the wonderful things the superstar could do. Next ask the child if she ever had a friend like that. You may want to describe how your friend helped you deal with such emotions as fear or jealousy. To build up your superstar, model him after the "Bionic Man" or some other superhero.

If the child had an imaginary friend, find out when the friend arrived and went away. Perhaps it was when you moved to a new house, or when the baby came and the child felt lonely and so fashioned a make-believe companion. Ask the child what kind of imaginary friend she could create that would help her out of trouble with you and what sort of imaginary friend would make it easier for her to deal with a nightmare.

22

Finders
Keepers

OBJECTIVE:
DREAMER'S IDEA
OF PROPERTY

One drizzly afternoon, Erin came clomping home from nursery school sporting a red "Snoopy" boot on one foot and a black galosh on the other. The galosh was hers; to whom the red boot belonged was anyone's guess—probably to a classmate. There was no way of talking Erin into returning the boot. She was hooked on Snoopy. As far as she was concerned, anything left unguarded with a picture of this famous pooch on it was hers under the law of "finders keepers."

Basically, this law works to satisfy the yearnings of very young children. With a vivid imagination, property lines can become blurred and a child can easily convince herself that if she can get her hands on the coveted object, it's hers. Finders keepers is essentially a form of wish fulfillment.

Don't believe for a second that this law would have held any water with the rightful owner of the Snoopy boot. If caught red-handed while taking the boot, Erin might have defended herself by saying it was a mistake—"I have one just like it at home." To be sure, she had boots at home, but hers were black galoshes. Obviously her boots were as different from the Snoopy ones as day is to night. But if a child wants something badly enough, her mind will go along and gloss over any differences. This glossing is done on impulse. Since there is no forethought or preplanning involved, I call this "impulse buying." It can't be classed as stealing unless there's intent. However, there is intent in "borrowing." When "borrowing," the dreamer makes little pretense that the object is hers. She is merely using it for "a while." The object will soon be returned or discarded, but never kept as if it were her own. "Borrowing" borders on stealing if the child keeps the object for a long time and takes pains trying to hide it.

Stealing occurs when the youngster takes something without the slightest notion of bringing it back. However, there are times when stealing is done for a noble cause. Once Erin took a neighbor's canary and let it go so it would be "free."

To determine the nature of your child's thinking on property and stealing, you can use the episode of Erin's freeing the canary. Ask the child the following questions: If the bird had been out of the cage, would it then have been all right for Erin to make it fly away? If the owner had been cruel to the bird, should Erin have set it free? Would it have been wrong if she had just left the cage door open so the canary could escape? Could Erin have mistaken the neighbor's canary for hers? Maybe Erin just wanted to borrow the bird for a while and then return it. Why was it wrong to let the bird go? What if no one saw Erin do it? What if she let the bird go and then brought it back? If she had always wanted a bird of her own and had never gotten one, would it have been all right for her to have taken this one?

DIARY:

CHAPTER

II

THE
POET
STAGE

3-5 YEARS OLD

One afternoon Christopher came flying home at such a clip that if the door had been barred, he probably would have bulled right through it. Huffing and puffing, he shot around the living room like Geronimo circling a wagon train, all the while yelling, "Daddy, Daddy, the big doggie tasted me!" As it turned out, Christopher had merely been licked by Alice, an overstuffed basset hound.

Why the word *taste* instead of *lick*?

You have to understand that the stage of creativity of the poet is filled with melodrama. It is a time when the youngster expresses not only the facts of what he's experiencing, but the emotions as well. The latter are often so highly charged that the facts are shoved into the background where, unexpressed, they are forgotten.

Christopher used *taste* to convey not the facts of reality, but the feelings that sprang from them: fear *and* joy. Apparently on first running into Alice, Christopher had been scared stiff, sensing he was about to be eaten alive. Hence the connection with taste. Yet when licked, Christopher rightly took this to mean he was liked in the sense that one likes things that taste good. Thus he used *taste* to convey his fear as well as his feeling of joy at being well liked.

Licked simply would not have done the job. Even if Christopher had been fluent enough to rattle off something like "I was afraid the dog was going to bite me, but he licked me instead," such a flat statement would never have carried the emotional punch packed into the single word *taste.*

Unfortunately, there aren't always words to express one's feelings, especially if they're mixed or double feelings as were Christopher's. But this never troubled the poet at all. He simply made up his own words to express his mixed emotions. Actually, as we have just seen, these are ordinary words whose definitions have been twisted to fit the poet's mood.

If you ever get the urge to correct the poet, bite your tongue. Remember that as a dreamer the youngster had to sift through hundreds of images, searching for the right one to communicate his experiences. Now he can reduce all these images to one word and is free to speak his mind. In this sense, the one word is worth a thousand pictures.

The ability to invent new words doesn't blossom overnight. It is a long, drawn-out process. At first the poet simply stews in his inability to pinpoint the right word. Next comes a sense that he's on the verge of something big. During this time, the mind subconsciously works overtime on the problem. Then without warning, the dam bursts. Lights flash and bulbs go off in the poet's head as the word or idea streaks across his mind in a burst of insight. It is his masterpiece. The poet is now able to communicate his dreams, a condition that rarely existed during the dream stage of creativity.

As one can imagine, the poet is flying sky-high. He is so agog with excitement that he wants to put life into everything he touches or says. Note Christopher's Oscar-winning takeoff of Geronimo. The poet is a born ham. He's a public figure and, as such, bears little resemblance to the dreamer, who more often than not is caged in his own private world. This is not to disparage dreaming; it's the source of all our ideas. Without dreaming, the poet would have nothing to express. But the poet does more than just express; he puts his own personal brand on things, as Christopher did with the word *taste*. The poet feels he's special. Artur Rubinstein, one of this century's most distinguished pianists, expressed the poet's feeling when he said, "If they say I play like a second Liszt or a second Paderewski or a second...then I'm wrong. If I'm second I'm an imitator not an artist. An artist is always himself."

It is difficult enough for a great artist, let alone a young poet, always to be himself. Though the youngster has made great strides, all is not smooth sailing. Built into the poetic stage is a lot of tension and frustration. You can't skirt it because it involves people speaking two different languages: the poet's personal vocabulary versus the adult's logical one. It's crushing to the poet not to have his efforts appreciated. Such a letdown often drives the poet into becoming a very grouchy and hard-to-handle youngster. But the biggest blow to his poetic ego or sense of being special is yet to come. It is delivered by a band of psychologists whose pet theory is that for the sake of clarity children should expand their vocabularies rather than condense their language into one-word masterpieces. This theory goes completely against the grain of the poet, who doesn't want to copy anyone or anything, let alone someone else's idea of language. He is an artist, not an imitator. And indeed, what's the rush? Expansion naturally comes about on its own during the inventive stage. Unfortunately, rather than wait, these psychologists have waged war on the poet's language, labeling it telegraphic, if not egocentric, speech.

Today there's a new philosophy in the air, which boils down to this: When a child is not up to snuff, when you really have to roll up your sleeves and work hard just to understand him, then the only solution is that the child must change; he is the one who is in error. Within educational circles there seems to be an increasing number of theories that cater more to adult convenience than to child development.

Having knocked his head against the wall trying to get his way, the poet in desperation turns to self-centeredness. This is his last-ditch effort to stand up to your attacks on his way of life. While this defense does stop you from tampering with his inner thoughts, it also prevents the poet's feelings from reaching the surface and being expressed. If the poet's feelings suffer at the cost of emphasis on facts, then whatever imagination the child has will be channeled into logical and scientific interests. The key to stimulating artistic talent lies in encouraging the child to express his emotions. If facts and emotions are given equal play, then chances are the child will feel at home in the arts as well as in the sciences—leaving you nothing more creative to deal with than the potential of a pint-sized Leonardo da Vinci.

You will have but a brief vacation from the poetic stage because it steals the scene once again from the early teens through the mid-twenties, roughly paralleling Erikson's stage of identity. In this return to the poetic stage, the poet's mind is, if anything, even more clouded. It's not enough that the adolescent poet has trouble making his feelings understood; on top of this, he's also shouldering an identity crisis. The adolescent poet and his younger counterpart share certain characteristics:

Insightfulness: The poet has flashes of insight that produce masterpieces.

Expressiveness: He is able to get things out in the open even if they're not always understood.

Grouchiness and self-centeredness: These are the poet's reactions to being constantly misunderstood.

Outgoingness and public orientation: The poet becomes really keyed up at being able to express himself.

Crisis of artistic vs. scientific creativity: The artistic side may be blocked if the poet's emotions aren't appreciated or grasped.

1

Diarrhea, Diphtheria, and **Dr. Seuss**

OBJECTIVE:
USING RHYMES
INTELLECTUALLY
AND CREATIVELY

The language kids pick up is funny and sometimes embar-
rassing. At around age three, Erin brought home the word *diarrhea*,
but she thought it meant "dear Rita" and proceeded to use it at

once with her Aunt Rita. What really took the cake was that she soon latched on to the word *diphtheria* and automatically applied that to her uncle.

Though "Diarrhea and Diphtheria" continued to visit us, they were never as close to Erin as they had once been. Maybe it was because they started having their own youngsters, or maybe it was Erin's salutation. But no matter how much we urged, Erin wouldn't drop her terminology. Eventually we stopped insisting, because for Erin both *diarrhea* and *diphtheria* were terms of affection and endearment. But just as important, to her the terms seemed to rhyme.

Rhyming is an intellectual exercise. It is the way young children practice and test out language, which is why *Dr. Seuss* ranks so high with kids. Something that doesn't rank so high with grown-ups are dirty words. However, for the preschooler, dirty words are often merely part of a rhyming scheme—"hit, bit, sh.."; so try not to overreact or your kids will catch on and spray out streams of dirty words solely for shock value. The thing to do is offer them substitutes for their rhyming scheme—"hip, lip, ship," or "hit, bit, lit."

Along with being an intellectual function, rhyming is also part of one's creative life, as evidenced by the use of rhymes in poetry.

To foster both the intellectual and creative side of the child, try the following rhyming activity: Call out a word that the child knows, such as her name, your name, or the name of a favorite toy, and ask her to say another word that sounds like the one you just used. Next you may want to make up a nonsense word—for example, *glockloby*—and see if she can make up her own nonsense word to rhyme with it.

DIARY:

2

Sound
Effects

OBJECTIVE:
FOSTERING
IMAGINATIVE SPEECH

Like all kids, ours loved commercials. Erik was crazy over "Fizz-Fizz-Plop-Plop," a TV jingle for selling a headache remedy. But he would only recite it when ensconced in one place, the toilet. Accompanying every bowel movement, you'd hear our merry little three-year-old belting out a stanza of "Fizz-fizz-plop-plop. Oh, what a relief it is!"

Obviously, one can put two and two together to see the connection between the sound effects rendered and Erik's mission in the bathroom. However amusing, this was not merely child's play, for such sound effects are the basis of onomatopoeia, a literary device for inventing imaginative words to represent sounds (for example, cling, clang, buzz, hiss). Besides displaying imaginative thinking, the sound effects also point to another important development: The child is beginning to express his mental images.

The following activity will help your youngster invent imaginative sound words (onomatopoeia): Ask him if he'd like to play a game that requires turning off the sound portion of one of his TV programs. Then ask him the sounds he hears when certain things happen on the show. What sound does that bee make? How does the snake sound? What sound does a speeding car make when it passes you? These questions require that the youngster translate whole pictures of mental images into scenes, or at least into the sounds associated with the images. Soon he'll be able to break down the images into different parts and then to represent each part or idea with words in sentences. However, at this point, he uses sound effects rather than specific words to convey his thoughts and internal images.

DIARY:

3

The
Breakfast
War

OBJECTIVE:
CONTROLLING ACTIONS
THROUGH LANGUAGE

Most kids use breakfast time as a time to eat. Christopher, however, used it as a time to retreat into fantasy. Around his place mat he'd slide cereal boxes, milk cartons, and jelly jars to make a private wall behind which to play. Then as he ate, he might pretend his spoon was a dive bomber or that the last cheerio in his bowl was the lone survivor of a *Titanic* type of disaster. Whatever the fantasy, it exploded into action as soon as Christopher started talking to himself, "Watch it, Joe! Not now. It's going to blow!" At this stage of play, he'd automatically wave his arms and dive under the table while in the process of spilling his breakfast.

It was amazing to see Christopher get so carried away with play once he began talking to himself. One was left with the impression that his ideas were bottled up under pressure and that once the ideas were released through words, his language just took over his actions.

We found that if you could get Christopher talking very early in his play before his ideas built up speed and pressure, his actions were more controlled, which resulted, among other things, in less spills at the table. The more a youngster talks to himself, the more his thinking becomes conscious and under the control of his language. Adults do it when they're stuck on a problem. Poets do it when an idea fails and they must lay the idea out in front of them where it can be reanalyzed and made to work. Adults call it going back to the drawing board; for kids, it's simply thinking and talking out loud. Even when done in the company of friends, such talking is not meant to communicate with anyone other than oneself. Psychologists label this talking without an intent to communicate a *collective monologue.*

To get your child to think out loud, show him some magazine pictures and then ask him to tell you what the characters in the pictures are saying. Try to find action pictures. While looking at the pictures, the child has to be thinking about or interpreting what's going on, so you are in fact asking him to translate his interpretation into words. As the words flow, do you notice an increase in his body movement? For many children, the process of putting thoughts into words is accompanied by an increase in physical activity. In a way, they're acting out their spoken thoughts.

DIARY:

4

The Chatter Box

OBJECTIVE:
STIMULATING
LANGUAGE FLOW

"You're going to marry me." (Silence.) "Yeeeeessss you are!" "NOPE." (Astonished pause.) "No? Is that what you said? You better! I'm going to get you! I'm going to tell. You just better marry me!"

Sound like a spiel from a soap opera? Although you would never recognize it as such, the spiel is actually the dialogue of two five-year-olds taking a language test. In fact, as far as tests go, at least from appearances, this one would not resemble anything you have ever seen because our test is a big box. To be more precise, it is an old refrigerator carton. Old as it is, the box has provided a new way of looking at language development.

The mystique between kids and boxes casts a magic spell that keeps kids playing for hours. But more than just stimulating play, boxes also trigger off virtually every type of language pattern available to the young child. Like Piaget with his little games of playing marbles and sorting buttons, we used the box to explore the child's world of language. In effect, the box has been the one setting to which most kids flock and speak their minds; hence, the name of our test, the "Chatter Box."

The Chatter Box started out as a seventy-by-forty-inch refrigerator carton whose outside and inside walls are painted in detail to depict a castle. One wall had a hatch cut out for the door. Within the box, there were appropriate props—paper swords, shields, and crowns. Although we chose the castle motif for our box, one could use any theme—pirate ship, rocket, submarine, cave dwelling, and so on—providing one developed it in the same rich detail and realism as the castle.

The box was like a magic curtain; once behind it the kids' language took off on imaginative sprees, especially their sentences. Inside the box, sentences tended to be long and involved ("Did you see that over there by the dragon before she dueled him?") in contrast to the dry, short, straight-to-the-point sentences typically uttered outside the box ("Stop!" "Do it." "Can I come?").

Generally the number of words in children's sentences runs something like this: Between ages two and three children use three-word sentences; between ages three and four, four-word sentences; and between ages four and five, five-word sentences. One activity is to keep track of sentence length inside and outside the Chatter Box.

A second activity is to gauge the complexity of the sentences. Do you find temporal clauses ("We'll hit the ball *before* it goes in the hole.")? Causal clauses ("That's all *because* it's broken.")? Conditional clauses ("You'll get in trouble *if* you hit him.")? Final clauses ("Take away the music *so that* I can sleep.")?

Yet another activity is to note the parts of speech found in the sentences. In the sentences of younger children, there are usually more verbs, some nouns, while adjectives and adverbs are sparse.

DIARY:

5

Commands

OBJECTIVE:
GIVING DIRECTIONS
AND
STORING INFORMATION

It seemed that since the day he learned to talk, Christopher always had to add his two cents to everything. Many a comment got him into hot water. Once on a crowded elevator, he asked to be put down to stand alone where he was only as tall as most adults' waists. You can imagine the general embarrassment when, after a fit of sniffing and snorting, he remarked, "Something smells down here!" Everyone turned red, fixed their eyes to the ceiling, and couldn't wait for the next stop. As soon as it came, there was a beeline to the door amid a flurry of murmurs, "Whose kid is that?" "I don't know, but they deserve each other!"

Despite all the trouble it stirred up, Christopher's kibitzing was amusing—until he was around four years of age when he started tagging commands onto each comment. We flew off the handle and started barking out our own orders like drill sergeants to a raw recruit: "Do it this way! Do it that way! Stop at once!" This state of affairs would have continued if it hadn't dawned on us that Christopher's commands might be signaling certain changes in his development, as indeed they were. Being in the poetic stage, Christopher was exploding with great ideas of better ways to do things (at least he thought they were great) and was trying to communicate these ideas to us. Unfortunately, in his zeal to communicate, his ideas came out sounding like commands. To make matters worse, his ideas were seldom accepted, which he so resented that he delivered his commands in a form that was all the more biting and caustic.

Remember that the child becomes frustrated when no one listens to his ideas, which he thinks are the greatest, and try to avoid locking horns with him. Keep in mind that in his earlier stage of development, the child merely kept his ideas to himself, except on those occasions when he slipped and thought or talked out loud, and that he is now trying to communicate with you.

Having a toy to handle helps children to communicate. The following activity should help your child with communicating and storing information: Ask him to explain how to put a puzzle together. Can he give you reasons for the directions he's giving? Ask him to evaluate the puzzle. Is it good or bad, and why?

DIARY:

6

Tattletale

OBJECTIVE:
DEVELOPING
CREATIVE FOCUS

Erin had perfect timing. As soon as one flopped down into a nice easy chair and before one could sip a drink or switch on the evening news, she would start her whining. "I'm tellin'. 'Top it. You took mine. Give me that. Don't call me bad names."

I could ignore it at first, until it built to such a pitch that I'd break out of the chair like an old racehorse going for broke, fuming at Erin while doing everything to stop myself from putting her two tormentors, Erik and Christopher, into perpetual orbit. I'd really lash into the boys telling them how much bigger and older they were and how they shouldn't frustrate poor Erin. In reality, however, it was Erin who was doing the frustrating. In fact, the closer one looked at things, the clearer it became that Erin was out to get my dander up with her tattling. Apparently, if either brother crossed her during the day, she knew just how to set me off to get back at them—quite a cunning strategy, and worth keeping in mind whenever you're dealing with cute, defenseless little four-year-olds.

Tattling, however, is more than a manipulative technique: it is one of the first forms of criticism. To criticize entails a standard. Earlier the child merely issued commands at whim, but at this point she has standards, the violation of which causes her to react with criticism. This signals definite progress. The standards act as a switch to cut off ideas that don't bear on the matter at hand. Developmentally the child moves from sound effects to talking to herself, to commands, to criticism. Her speech and thoughts are much more specific, as are her creative ideas, which now have considerably more focus and relevance.

One way to foster this creative focus is to have the child work on similes. If she's criticizing someone for being slow, you may say, "Erik is as slow as a turtle." Another possibility is to use similes as compliments, which is the opposite form that criticism can take:

He's as fast as _____ .

I'm as tall as _____ .

You're as pretty as _____ .

That's as big as _____ .

DIARY:

7

"Why Do Ducks Wear Rubbers?"

OBJECTIVE:
EVALUATING "WHY"
QUESTIONS

On first hearing Erin's duck question, my mind shook like an overstuffed computer with circuits popping and lights flashing out the message: "MISINFORMATION—CORRECT MISINFORMATION—CORRECT." Luckily, before I could ruin things, Erik stepped in and suggested, "They're like frogmen."

My kids were speaking in a language alien to adults, which I call "Kreation." Kreation teems with metaphors, such as "ducks wearing rubbers," and also with similes like the one Erik used to answer Erin's question. Both are creative expressions and both are difficult enough for adults to understand, let alone create.

All languages have their favorite idioms. For Kreation, the favorite idiom is "why" questions. Such questions can't be taken at face value. They must be interpreted. What follows is an interpretative guide, divided into stages, which should help us understand some of the reasons behind our kids' questions.

GUIDE

Basis of Question	Example	Reason	Response
		STAGE 1: DREAMER	
Surprise	"Why is the dragon green?"	The child is startled. Something has not met his expectations. This question is in fact an emotional reaction.	No logical answer is needed; instead, soothe the child.
Rhetoric	"Why is the dragon green?"	The child's egocentric mind has produced its own answer.	No answer is required.
Politeness	"Why should I touch the dragon?"	This "why" question is a polite way of saying "no."	Reasoning seldom works. Try flattery.
		STAGE 2: POET	
Confirmation	"Why did I see a green dragon?"	The child is growing out of realism and wants you to reinforce that what he sees is real and not something he created in his imagination.	"You did see a green dragon."

Basis of Question	Example	Reason	Response
Motives	"Why is the dragon green?"	The child assumes that animals, like humans, have motives.	"He likes to scare people."
Maker	"Why is the dragon green?"	The child may be seeking primary causes.	"God made him that way." "His mommy made him like that."

STAGE 3: INVENTOR

Basis of Question	Example	Reason	Response
Purpose	"Why is the dragon green?"	This could be a case of teleological reasoning—that is, the child is searching for a final cause or purpose.	"To hide in the jungle."
Chance	"Why is the dragon green?"	The child has just discovered universal laws, or that there is an explanation for everything. At this point, any answers you give will get a thousand "whys" in return. It will drive you mad. Nothing will shut him up. Everything must have a reason. (e.g., "Why is today called Tuesday and not Monday?")	"Because" works well in most cases since this word represents for the child a law in and of itself.

Basis of Question	Example	Reason	Response
Causality	"Why is the dragon green?"	Here the child is demanding an elaborate and deductive explanation.	"The dragon is green because it can hide in the jungle. If it were brown, it couldn't hide and then it would be killed."

This guide demonstrates the complexity of young children's thinking. It would be obviously impossible to pinpoint the right answer for every question, but you can go halfway by gearing your answers to "why" questions to fit the child's developmental stage:

DREAMER: As the guide points out, "why" questions in this stage usually take care of themselves.

POET: Humanize your answer: "The duck's mommy makes her wear rubbers."

INVENTOR: Try analogies: "Ducks are like frogmen; they spend a lot of time in the water."

If your answer is "hot" or on target, the child will usually comment on it. Once this happens, the ice is broken and the youngster is more likely to reveal the reasons behind her questions. When you humanize your answers, do you get more questions? What generally happens when the child hears your analogies? What are some of the child's comments? What do the comments relate to?

DIARY:

8

The Longest Walk

OBJECTIVE:
KNOW HOW
TO ANSWER
QUESTIONS

How long does it take to walk three blocks? Ten or fifteen minutes? Cover the distance with Christopher and you'll be lucky to do it in an hour. Why? That's it exactly—you will be peppered with thousands of questions: "where," "what," and "how."

Since kids seem to thrive on asking such questions, we'll deal with each type separately.

"Where" questions pop up during the dreamer stage. At this point, although the child is absorbed in his private world of fantasy, he can manage some curiosity over the disappearance of people and things into their own private and hidden places. That curiosity is one reason for such questions as: "Where does night go?" "Where does the wind go?" "Where you going?" "Where's Mama?"

The last two questions about the destination and absence of people show that "where" questions are tied to the child's need for security and belonging. Not wishing to lose those he cherishes, the youngster consistently tries to keep track of their every move. Awareness of the reasons behind these questions might make them easier to handle and tolerate, especially on days when you're running out of patience.

"What" questions really take hold during the poetic stage. As the child plies his thoughts in the real world, he runs into many discoveries, one of which is that everything has a name. Hence, the questions: "What's that for?" "What's that called?" "What day is it now?" Labels improve the child's ability to form associations.

Finally, "how" questions typify the stage of invention. At this time, the child is intrigued with how most things work, which leads to such questions as: "How does the sun go down?" "How does water go uphill?" "How do stars stay up?"

The problem with questions is not getting them asked, for nothing short of gagging a four-year-old will stop his questioning. The trouble comes in trying to answer the child, since he's basically intuitive and isn't always reaching for adult explanations. One tack is to turn the question around and have the child answer it. Such a procedure can open one's eyes to the intuitive combinations and inventive associations of a young creative mind.

Adult	Child
"Christopher, *you* answer the question. Where do *you* think the night goes?"	"In the black sewer, Mom."

Adult   **Child**

(This is a *visual* association. Christopher has seen a likeness between the darkness of night and that of a sewer.)

"Christopher, what's a knife?"   "It's the spoon's husband."

(This is a *spatial* association: Knives and forks are usually placed next to each other, like a married couple.)

"Christopher, how do *you* think stars   "From milk splats."
are made?"

(Our little boy had just seen a cake batter being stirred and as the beads of milk flew out of the mixing bowl, he asked about the stars. This is a *temporal* association of two things happening close in time.)

The best approach to "where," "what," and "how" questions seems to be (1) turning the questions around and having the child answer them; and (2) after getting a feeling for the workings of his imaginative mind, answering his questions on the basis of the visual, spatial, and temporal associations mentioned above. Does the dreamer seem to prefer a visual association? Which one does the poet prefer? What type of question does your child ask the most? What are the hardest questions to answer?

DIARY:

9

Arguments

OBJECTIVE:
DE-CENTERING

How would you like your weekend spoiled by a plump baby stuffed into a pink Dr. Denton suit? (Dr. Denton's are one-piece pajamas that fit as snugly as body suits.)

To me, the baby looked like a fully packed sausage, but I would never have ventured my opinion since it was her very appearance that touched off the feud that blew the weekend: Christopher insisted she was a pink dog, while Erik wouldn't budge from his opinion that she was a big rabbit. Both could have been right since this particular Dr. Denton suit came equipped with a long dog tail and a hood sporting two peaks that might easily have been rabbit ears.

Though we had little luck in cooling the boys' tempers, we did notice certain clues that signaled the escalation of the argument. The clues occurred at different levels of argument, as can be seen below:

Levels	Example
1. Debating: The words deal only with the problem. Nothing is personal.	"Did you ever see a rabbit with a long tail?"
2. Insulting: Words are used for teasing and taunting, which signals that things are becoming personal.	"Christopher, you're a dog dummy! Dog dummy, dog dummy! Na-na! Dog dummy."
3. Quarreling: The words now contain physical threats and commands and are backed up by menacing gestures.	"Don't call me that. I'm going to punch you!"
4. Fighting: The words are dropped and acts of physical aggression take over.	Biting, pulling hair, clawing, kicking, and so forth.

These are the general levels of childrens' arguments. Children can be sidetracked while operating on the second level ("insulting"), but once into "quarreling," they are too impassioned and are beyond any control other than physical restraint. By tracking the levels, it is possible to nip arguments in the bud, or at least to keep them on the level of teasing and taunting. At that level, youngsters are still open to reason and suggestion.

Many feuds, including the one that Christopher and Erik had, stem from *centering*, which is a way of thinking peculiar to the young mind. To "center" is to make a decision about an object by taking into consideration only one of its parts and leaving out the rest. Christopher, for example, zeroed in on the tail, while Erik saw only the ears.

Try this activity to help your child de-center: Cut into pieces some magazine ads showing men and women. Arrange the pieces so that they form a contradictory picture—for example, paste the head of a woman to the burly torso of a man and have one arm wielding a baseball bat while the other cradles a baby. Finally, cover the legs with a skirt and put work shoes on the feet. Quickly flash the picture in front of the child and ask him what it is. If he answers a man (or a woman), ask him about the factors on which he based his decision. Point out that it could have been a woman (or man) if he based his decision on some other parts of the picture. Does the child become more, or less, confused as the picture is exposed for longer periods of time? If he gets more confused, he is still centering. The longer time should have helped him reason out the contradiction (for example, "It has to be a man because he could have long hair, but a girl could never have a chest like that.").

DIARY:

10

The
Garbled
Message

OBJECTIVE:
DEALING WITH
EGOCENTRIC SPEECH

When the phone rang around our place, it was every man for himself. You'd swear it was the Oklahoma land rush, but instead of pioneers staking out sections of Mother Earth, all the commotion was stirred by our kids scrambling to see who could get to Ma Bell first. Even after the phone was secured, the scrambling continued, as was evidenced by the garbled phone messages that were relayed. Erik was the worst offender. Once when we were selling our house, he got to the phone first and relayed this tangled message: "She said the house cost a lot. No, no—the lot cost ... I don't know. Just call her where she is when she comes from there with the chicken."

No thanks to Erik, we sold the house pretty quickly, but it was a long time before our boy got his lines straight. His problem was *egocentric speech*. Though he could understand things, he couldn't communicate them very well.

Egocentric speech is the language of the poetic stage. Caught up in their own little worlds, young children rarely take the time to translate their thoughts into clear terms. Erik's shorthand message is a good example of this kind of speech. Though *he* knew what "she," "where," "when," "there," *we* were left in the dark.

Part of the child's problem is that he has an irresistible urge to speak his thoughts. Therefore he just stampedes through anyone else's thoughts or messages. For an activity that helps cut down on egocentric speech, try making up stories with your child. When an adult and a child have something to share that's personally important to both of them, the child usually becomes more exacting in his language.

Start the story by giving the *theme*: "A policeman is outside your window." Ask the child for the *plot*, or what happens next. Toward the end of the story, state the *climax*: "Someone falls out the window." Finally, have the child *resolve* the story. During the plot, does the child fumble around, lost for ideas? This may signal egocentric thinking. Tell him to talk out what he's thinking (see activity 3 in this chapter). Fidgeting or squirming is a sign that the child's ideas have begun to jell. The child wants to be sure that his thinking is clear, so this activity may take time. How does the child handle the resolution? Is it connected to the rest of the story? A logical connection should be stressed.

11

Jokes

OBJECTIVE:
STIMULATING CREATIVE ASSOCIATIONS

One afternoon while Erin was playing far off in the living room corner, I was watching TV when the announcer mentioned that evening's late movie, *The Mouse That Roared*. In a flash, Erin was at my side with a puzzled look and a question, "Mouse woars, not yion woar?" I nodded yes, which sent her into gales of laughter. Seldom had I seen a three-year-old carry on so over simply hearing a few words. With most children of this age, it's the sheer physical joy of fast running and free jumping that gives rise to such laughter. Not until age four or five do words, jokes, music, friends, and other social stimuli touch off the kind of belly laugh that Erin was experiencing.

Occasionally a three-year-old may crack up over a slapstick routine or a practical joke, such as scaring someone with a loud "BOO!" The appeal of both these forms of humor rests in the momentary advantage they provide the child over someone big or powerful. Later, during the school years, laughter becomes a shock absorber for cushioning the stings of disappointment, frustration, and other psychological setbacks.

However, Erin's laughter over a mouse that roared stemmed from something else; her newfound ability to appreciate incongruity. She was now able to see the absurdity in certain situations and to accept it. Earlier her thinking had been much too rigid to go along with such a playful combination as a roaring mouse. This flexibility and playfulness of thought signaled that Erin was ready to form unusual combinations of associations, a major step in creative thinking.

One way to tap into the child's sense of humor, and at the same time to strengthen her creative associations, is to make up some flip-flop statements: "The doggie goes meow." "The fish ran across the street." "The sun shines at night." "The father wore a diaper." Does your child find these funny? Does she find certain flip-flops involving certain types of dogs, ducks, fathers, and so on, funnier than others? If you give the child the stem ("The cat goes _____"), can she add the tag line? Does the child begin to make up her own flip-flops?

DIARY:

12

Lies

OBJECTIVE:
INVESTIGATING REALISM
AND INVENTION

We had not been in our new home for more than a week when a tiny boy came to the door with Erik in tow and asked, "Does his dog really read?"

This was just one of the little fibs Erik had planted on his new friends to impress them. Though youngsters stretch the truth for many reasons—to startle, to flatter, to keep secrets, or, like Erik, to brag—they seldom lie to mislead willfully, as do adults.

Adult lies have one motive, to deceive. Children's lies stem from two motives, neither of which is to deceive. The first is "realism," or self-deception. If the child thinks about or wishes for something long enough, he finally believes it to be fact. The second motive is "invention," and it comes into play when the child finds that no one can tell the difference when he changes facts or rearranges ideas (like having a dog that reads). In some situations, his inventions are even accepted as truth.

In handling our children's lies, we used the following guidelines: (1) Never *expose* the child in front of his friends. (2) When alone, *probe* for the motive ("Why do you need a dog that reads?" "So the kids would really like me."). (3) Provide *substitutes*—for example, a list of things the child actually has that would make him attractive to his friends. Fortunately, the ability to rearrange ideas is channeled into other areas, such as the formation of playful associations or combinations, which is the heart of creative thinking.

A good activity to help channel this ability is to ask your child "if" questions. Such questions require the child to deal with hypothetical or imaginary situations: "If your birthday didn't come this year, what would you do?" "If the sun fell from the sky, what would you do?" "If you found a candy tree, what would you do?" How does the child handle these questions? Realistically? Fancifully? Can he make up "if" questions?

DIARY:

13

Colors

What do these words have in common: *nine, sharp,* and *slippery*? Some sort of a time schedule or curfew, you might guess. Maybe for you that's their meaning, but for Christopher they were the definition of *green*. For most three-year-olds, the naming of colors sets off feelings and images associated with experiences that have touched them deeply. In short, kids use colors to communicate emotions in much the same way adults use such figures of speech as "green with envy" or "he's feeling blue."

Though Christopher knew his colors, he found them of little use in discriminating between objects. A red ball was the same as a yellow, blue, or white one; they were all round, smooth, and capable of rolling, regardless of color. The ability to deck out experiences in bright colors is called *synaesthesis*. Artists, writers, and musicians keep this ability sharp and sensitive so that whenever they encounter a unique sight, taste, or sound, their minds can fire off a rainbow of vivid images.

The child's imaginative bent for learning isn't limited to words. The same process operates in many areas, even one as standardized as classifying. One youngster was shown pictures of three vegetables (a carrot, tomato, and pepper) and one of a fruit (lemon). When asked which picture did not belong, he replied, "The tomato." Asked if there were any others, he responded, "The carrot." In the third go-around, he finally mentioned the lemon. His first two answers weren't incorrect because when questioned, he revealed an interesting classification system: His first response was an emotional classification, "I hate tomatoes"; his second response was based on the reasoning that "carrots grow underground like roots."

The child's reasoning operates on three levels: (1) emotional reasoning ("I hate tomatoes"); (2) personal logic ("they're like roots"); and (3) standard logic, such as an adult would use in selecting the lemon. These levels correspond with the three stages of creativity: The dreamer stage corresponds to emotional reasoning; the poet stage to personal logic; and the inventor stage to standard logic. To see how many different levels of reasoning your child is operating on, set up a number of classification activities involving one item that doesn't belong.

DIARY:

14

"Earthquakes
Are the Baddest"

OBJECTIVE:
IMPROVING YOUNG
CHILDREN'S
GRAMMAR

One evening the national TV news included a feature on the threat of earthquakes in California. As the feature ended, Erik whimpered, "I'm a-fade. They come here?" In a flash, Christopher rescued his brother with, "No, no, they're too big to come to our town. We're too small."

Apparently, Christopher figured Mother Nature wouldn't waste a spectacular performance on such a small, out-of-the-way place as ours when she had California to work on. Although Christopher's notion of Mother Nature was fascinating, there was something equally as intriguing in his reasoning, which was his concept of comparison: Big things happen in big places and little things in little places.

Christopher's ideas on comparison weren't limited to extraordinary natural phenomena. They were constantly springing up in his everyday conversations in such gems as, "he's badder," "she's worser," "that's the goodest." A purist would cringe over such usage if it were not that of a four-year-old. At this age, the child is full swing into poetic thinking, which renders him oblivious to, among other things, how words sound in the real world. The poet is only in tune with his own ideas, which he considers the "goodest." Currently, his ideas for making comparisons is to add "er" or "est" onto any word. Similarly, his idea for forming the past tense is to tag an "ed" onto verbs, which can result in such expressions as "he eated the bun" or "she drinked the juice."

As anyone who has logged time with preschoolers knows, all one's preaching on proper grammar makes little dent on their minds. A more effective strategy is to put the child in the company of some older playmates whom he admires. Using this strategy, one will soon begin to notice changes in the child's habits of speech.

One way to stimulate comparisons is to feed the child a rapid stream of phrases, such as: "The spoon is bigger than _____. The pig is smaller than _____. The tree is as green as _____." Keep in mind two points: (1) the types of comparison possible—weight, height, length, color, feel, taste, and so on; and (2) the objects being compared—people, animals, plants, rocks, tools, and so on. Can the child make comparisons with all objects? Is he stuck on one type of comparison (weight, length)? How is he at drawing equal comparisons? (For example, "The boat's as old as _____.")

15

Sparrow Gas

OBJECTIVE:
STIMULATING
ASSOCIATIONS

Have you ever had one of those days when you feel backed against the wall and ready to crack? And then when it finally looks as if you're going to get a breather by packing your last child off to Harold's party, your little darling, like Erin, pipes up, "I ain't going to Harold's. They make you eat yucky sparrow gas!" Did you fling her out of the car, gun the engine, and leave her stranded on Harold's doorstep? Or did you try to reason with her?

Obviously, speeding away was not the answer, but in this case neither was reasoning. Yet I persisted and started wading through a checklist. "Were they nuts that looked like bird seeds?" "Was it a coke or some other bubbly, gassy drink?" "What was it?" Instead of wasting time on this line of questioning, I should have gone with Erin into Harold's and had her point out what was so "yucky." This strategy would have quickly led me to the discovery that the offending item was nothing other than *asparagus.*

Asparagus is just one of the hundreds of tongue twisters three-year-olds get tied up with. There are several reasons for such miscues:

Auditory factors: The child fails to discern fine shades of differences. (Thus, *wasp* may come out sounding like *waps.*)

Emotional factors: A particular sound is stressed because of some personal association with the word (*holiday,* for example, is sometimes pronounced *holler-day* because of all the noise and excitement associated with the day).

Articulation: Some sounds are simply tricky for kids, so they make substitutions. Dental sounds made by pressing the tongue against the teeth are substituted for palatal sounds made with the tongue in the roof of the mouth: *good* becomes *dood, coffee can* becomes *toffe tan.*

Euphony: Children have a knack of giving words a certain pleasant sounding ring or rhythm. (The strong *g* in sugar turns the word to *gugar,* while the *t* of button turns it to *tutton.*)

It may seem to you that the child is primarily responsible for all these creative distortions. However, for many children, someone else's mention of certain explosive words can unleash a flood of associations. One of the best ways to stimulate your child's creative vocabulary is to reel off different words and then ask her all the things that come to mind with each word. What words spark the most associations in your child? Can you group these highly explosive words? Do most of them relate to animals, people, or things? Does a picture of the object uncork as many associations as the word?

16

Coining Words

OBJECTIVE: STIMULATING NEW TERMS

Some people may have allergies or hay fever, but to Erik such afflictions were all "flower colds." For that matter, toes were "foot fingers"; eyelids, "face curtains"; weather vanes, "wind tells"; and vending machine products, "punch candies."

The ability to invent words seems to reach its peak during the preschool years and then to diminish with age. Certainly, as adults we continue to make up new words, but they tend to be very technical and not descriptive of real things. For example, there are a number of terms, such as *dirigible* and *zeppelin*, to describe a blimp, but how do they stack up to one youngster's creation of *windship*?

This is not to say that all adult thinking is formal and dry. Ironically, it has been in physics, our most exact and technical field of knowledge, that researchers have coined a most unscientific-sounding term to describe the basic element of all matter: *quarks*. Interestingly, as we reach the frontiers of new knowledge, we seem not too far removed from the playful inventiveness of the preschooler.

There seem to be some objects just made to trigger off new words. Usually, these objects have color, make noise, or move. Let your child play with a little toy car that has a dull finish. Next give him a brightly painted toy car. Finally, roll the bright car down a small ramp. What is his reaction to the toys? Ask him what is going on in each situation. Is he more imaginative with the brightly colored rolling toy car? Does he talk out loud with any of the toys? Does he provide sound effects? Again, the more sounds and words the child uses, the more his ideas are charging and flowing at a faster rate. Such fast-moving ideas are a sign of the highly creative mind.

DIARY:

17

Learning
to Read

At three, Erin could read a dozen words. How she did this, we were never sure. In fact, one of the surest things about reading is that even the experts are not sure about how kids learn to read. As of now, there are three basic ways to teach reading: (1) the *phonics* approach, in which children are taught rules for attaching or breaking down words into meaningful sounds; (2) the *whole-*

word approach, in which a slight vocabulary is mastered by memorizing words on flash cards; and (3) the *linguistics* approach, in which the child's experiences are made into stories that she learns to read.

No approach has a 100 percent guarantee of teaching reading. So the best advice is to use the mixed-bag approach of combining all three methods. However, if your interest is less in teaching reading than in getting an idea of how the young mind is working while it is learning to read, the linguistic approach is most helpful.

In using this approach with Erin, we learned the experiences she used to master her word list. She learned *dog* because the *g* looked like a tail; *bed* because the *B* looked like two bumpy pillows; *look* because the double *oo*'s were two eyes; *Dave* because of a family friend, Big Dave, whose flexed biceps resembled a dome-shaped rim similar to the letter *D*.

"What's Your Favorite Letter or Number?" is a little game that all kids love to play. This game is a good way to gain insight into how different personal experiences influence a child's attraction to various words and letters. In asking the child her favorite letter, see if you can pinpoint any relationships. Does her favorite letter appear in the name of any person or place she likes? Is the letter part of a happy word, birthday, present, or candy? Perhaps the letter is one of a group that your little girl finds interesting. Some youngsters group letters into families: *y* and *g* may be in the tail family; *T, E,* and *F* in the hat family, while *P* and *R* are in the nose family. Does your child group letters into any of these families? Ask if certain letters or words have a bad, hungry, sleepy, or watery sound.

DIARY:

18

"Do Stomachs Have Teeth"

OBJECTIVE:
STIMULATING
EARLY LOGIC

Christopher had the unusual habit of being able to write with both hands. I say *unusual* because it's not abnormal for some kids not to settle on a dominant hand even up to the early grades in school. Still, I tried to get him to stick to one hand until one day when he looked me squarely in the eye and asked, "How come I have two eyes and can't see two things?" Since he could write with two hands, it seemed only natural to him to expect that he could see different things with two eyes. More than natural, it was logical, as was a whole new line of questioning that sprang up during his fifth year.

During this time, there wasn't a day when I wasn't pinned against the wall with such questions as, "Is there a Mrs. God?" "Do stomachs have teeth?" "When the first man was born, who was his mother?"

From these questions, it is clear that the child recognizes the logical inconsistencies in his world. Moreover, since there are many questions you can't answer, the child also suffers the shock of your inconsistency. In short, you are no longer seen as infallible, which is such a letdown to the child that it may cause a temporary strain in his relationship with you, especially if you tend to brush off his questions as inane or unimportant. This falling-out couldn't come at a worse time because the youngster is in transition between his magical years and logical years and needs your support to make this as smooth a move as possible; so stay cool, patient, and understanding.

The following activity is one way to foster your child's thinking: Put together two statements, one of which is inconsistent: "Terry plays for the Reds. He comes to the game dressed in green." (Is there anything wrong with the way Terry's dressed?) "The bear is eating honey, but the honey is dripping all over his feathers." (Do bears have feathers?) "Mary is watering her garden but can't find the tomatoes because they're covered with snow." (Would tomatoes grow in the snow?) Sometimes the child may see the inconsistency but may justify it. On other occasions, he may just flatly deny that such a thing as a "bear with feathers" exists. Are there some inconsistencies he can't detect? What are the ones he can live with? Which ones are most obvious to your child?

DIARY:

19

Fairy
Tales

OBJECTIVE:
DEVELOPING THE
CONCEPT OF
PROBABILITY OR CHANCE

"Do rocks bleed?" You could count on Erik to come up with such a question because he believed in *animism*, the notion that all things—stones, clouds, trees, rivers, not to mention animals— are alive and behave very much like human beings. But no one was ready for Christopher's answer, "No silly, that's a magic rock. It doesn't bleed."

If you have been following Christopher's progress, you know how quick he was to spot inconsistencies in the real world, so you too might have been caught off guard by his reply. However, though nearly six, Christopher was not a bit fazed by the irregularities found in fairy tales, whether they concerned singing swans, dancing elephants, or magic stones. Magic stones are in fact a feature of *Sylvester and The Magic Pebble*, one of Christopher's favorite stories. Despite the fact that Christopher was well into the stage of invention, he was, if anything, as hooked on fairy tales now as he had ever been.

Youngsters are drawn to fairy tales and childrens' stories for different reasons at different stages. "Realism," or the inability to distinguish between fact and fantasy, accounts for the dreamer's attraction to these stories, while it's animism that attracts the poet. The poet's imagination is also fueled by artificialism, the idea that the world is run by magicians and other superpowers who can be influenced through secret words or formulas. Often the secret words take the form of poems, as in *Winnie the Pooh*:

Cottleston, Cottleston, Cottleston Pie,
A fly can't bird, but a bird can fly.
Ask me a riddle and I reply:
"Cottleston, Cottleston, Cottleston pie."

At other times, they're found in such favorite formulas as, "Rain, rain go away..."; "One potato, two potato..."; "Eeny, meeny, miney, mo..."

The poet is trying to deal with the world logically and when this fails, he figures there must be other forces at play, notably superpowers with whom he must use secret words. What he misses is the idea that chance or luck may have entered the picture. However, at this stage, he has no inkling of such concepts. Yet, much of our scientific understanding of the real world is based on reasoning by probability or chance.

The following activity can give your youngster an idea of probability: Find seven patches of colored cloth—four red, two blue, and one white. (Any three colors will do just as long as they keep to the four-two-one combination.) Lay out all the patches and ask the child which one has the most colors. Then put all seven in an envelope and have the child guess which color he's going to pick as he blindly sticks his hand into the envelope. How many tries before he guesses red? When he picks a blue or white patch, how does he explain it? Ask the child what he would do to make the blue come out more. Does he reduce the number of red patches, increase the blue, or both? If he tries any of these approaches, he's showing an understanding of probability.

DIARY:

20

King Con

OBJECTIVE:
DISCIPLINING THE
CREATIVE CHILD

King "Con" isn't a forty-foot gorilla. Rather, he's a forty-inch con artist named Erik who just outfoxed old Dr. Kruper by locking himself in the good doctor's bathroom. Kruper, long on medical knowledge but short on patience, threatened to hammer down the bathroom door unless Erik came out to be zapped with a flu shot. This threat was immediately met with a roaring flush of the toilet, which almost drowned out Erik's reply, "I'm sowwy, I can't hear you."

Needless to say, our appointment had to be rescheduled. But Erik was not solely responsible for the day's undoing. I should never have let him get a locked door between us, but neither should Dr. Kruper have reacted as he did. Not that our boy didn't deserve it, but he was at an age when it was possible to get more from him with sugar than with anger. Erik coud now stand up much better for his rights in situations in which he had once felt helpless. When as a dreamer he was faced with something unpleasant, like a needle, he'd merely cry out, "Home, Dada. Home, Dada." The poet stage initially brought with it only self-centered defiance: "No, no. I bite you." But with time Erik had developed many more moves: stalling you with hundreds of irrelevant questions; talking his way out of jams; and if necessary, mocking you, "I'm sowwy, I can't hear you."

The child's growing sophistication in language is a signal that you should adopt different control techniques. Among the techniques that are possible are ultimatums ("Do it or you're going to bed."); negative commands ("Don't do that."); orders ("Clean that now."); requests, ("Please clean up."); suggestions ("I think it would work better this way."); analogies ("That's the way Batman does it."); reasons ("Do it that way so it won't drip.").

At this stage of his life, your child has three ways of getting around authority. He can draw on the dreamer's ploy of playing on your emotions, "It hurts too much, Daddy. Please take me home." Or there is the inventor's strategy of playing up his reasoning by asking you to justify your request (for example, to a request that he pick up his fork, Erik might respond, "Why can't I wait until after dinner? My food will get cold. Cold food makes me sick. You don't want me to throw up?"). Finally, there's always the poet's power play: "I won't do it. Make me."

True, some of these techniques of resistance were available to the child earlier in his development. But now with his sophisticated language, they can be expressed in adult terms, which leads to an interesting game between parents and children. You make a request. Your child counters with a power play. Now it's your move. Will you lead with an ultimatum? A reason? Another request? When the child was younger, he couldn't express his resistance in an adult manner so you treated him as a child. But at this point, since he can get his message across on your terms, you begin to treat him as an adult and start playing word games: He moves with a request. You counter with an order. He switches to a reason, and so on.

Here's an activity with which you can diagnose the game you and your child are playing. Set up the following grid. Can you piece together a pattern? How many of his power plays does it take before you move to a negative command? Does your boy have a favorite move? How does he get you to relent? Are there different patterns with different adults? Is the same game played at home and at school?

ADULT MOVES	CHILDREN'S MOVES		
	EMOTIONS (dreamer)	POWER (poet)	REASON (inventor)
REQUEST			
SUGGESTION			
ORDER			
NEGATIVE COMMAND			
ULTIMATUM			
ANALOGY			
REASON			

DIARY:

CHAPTER

III

THE INVENTOR STAGE

4-6 YEARS OLD

From the start Erik was always wiser than his years; yet, like all his playmates, he still hadn't developed the airtight logical thinking that separates the preschooler from the school-aged child. But now as an inventor, logic was to play a big role in his life. So much so that it would have been a big mistake to try to pull anything over on him. Though if you're nervy enough to try such a thing with an inventor, good luck. Just be ready to eat your words, as I did the night Erik and I got into the sticky subject of Santa Claus. There had been other occasions on which we had covered everything from God to babies. But on those occasions I had always been able to worm my way out of any tight spot by turning Erik's questions around on him. However, on this particular night my number was up. It was my turn to eat crow. Apparently Erik had caught on to my little trick and had neatly set aside a few key facts we had discussed in the past. So this time he was ready when I bounced his question back to him: "Son, what do *you* think about Santa Claus?" "Well," he answered, "If Santa brings gifts, the stork babies, and the Lord our daily bread, then what good are you, Daddy?"

I was utterly defeated. Intellectually, I should have been on guard because inventors are noted for blasting away at you with some heavy logical guns. Unlike the poet who is content merely to express his ideas, the inventor wants his ideas to be strong and workable in the real world. Because of this, he takes every opportunity to test his ideas against the toughest standards of logic he can find, which usually means you, the parent.

Reinforcing his powerful logic are three other new abilities: contiguity, closure, and similarity:

1. *Contiguity* is chain reaction thinking: Two or more ideas that are close in meaning overlap and something unique unfolds. Basically contiguity means fitting together ideas that normally don't go together but when presented in this unique combination suddenly seem to make sense. Erik came up with the term *electrifrying* to describe the burn he suffered from touching a live wire.
2. The best example of *closure* is puzzle play: The inventor is driven to fill in missing pieces and tie up loose ends, which is why he won't let anything come between him and the completion of his masterpiece.
3. *Similarity* is a shorthand term for analogous thinking. When Erik explained that "clouds move to get away from the hot sun," he was putting himself in the place of a cloud. Since Erik moves to seek shade, he attributed the same motive to the clouds.

Similarity, or putting himself in another's place, is a complete turnabout for the inventor. Closure is also a new development: the inventor will take any measures to get his masterpiece completed, whereas the poet would never have given up such ground. The poet feels that he sweated hard enough to come up with the idea; now it's your turn to work to understand it. With the inventor, it's a totally different picture. His mission is to help us understand, no matter what the sacrifice. Rodin, the great nineteenth-century sculptor, spent over twenty years on his classic *Portals of Hell* just to achieve the right balance and perspective. History is crammed with examples of such creative perseverance, as it is with stories of those whose genius was expressed more swiftly through poetic inspiration. Jules Verne possessed the latter type of talent. He dashed off material faster than the ink could dry on it. Though his imaginative ideas about flying were read by thousands of people, it was nearly half a century before the Wright brothers, two bicycle repairmen well-grounded in the nuts and bolts of mechanics, realized Verne's prophecy.

This emphasis on the inventor is not meant to disparage the poetic stage; it is our main source of inspiration and insight. However, once the unique idea has sprung, it must then be hammered into shape through compromise and much trial and error, which often lead to dead ends. Failure to benefit from his efforts drives the inventor into gloom, especially when he's still so close to the glamour and fire of the poetic stage. Only sheer willpower and guts keep the inventor on track. Without this stick-to-itiveness, one's creativity would never see the light of day. As the saying goes, "Genius is 99 percent perspiration and 1 percent inspiration." With all this hard work and sacrifice under his belt, it suddenly dawns on the inventor that his masterpiece has been chipped away to nothing; it bears scarcely any resemblance to his original idea.

Many of the chips in his masterpiece stem from the inventor's tendency to run his ideas first past his immediate family and then past anyone who will listen—school chums, aunts, uncles, teachers, and so on. This was never the style of the poet, who stuck mainly to an inner circle of family and friends. With this new style come some advantages; one in particular is that the inventor is hit with a ton of advice, some of which acts to shave and reshape his original idea. There is also a big disadvantage: All this information overloads the inventor's circuits, forcing him to slip back into his private world to rehash all that he's encountered. In doing so, the inventor appears moody. One moment he's the life of the party, pumping everyone for advice, and next he's crawling back into his shell. It's a tough time for the inventor. He's full of doubt because most of this advice is contradictory if not downright foreign to his original thinking. This is the hardest pill for him to swallow. He'll never be able to complete the masterpiece and blames himself for the failure.

Self-criticism never helps creativity. If anything, it's a sure way to kill it. Parents and teachers can step in to bolster the inventor's self-image before his confidence falls completely to pieces. Fortunately, however, along with the altered self-image of the inventor, there does *not* come an overwhelming sense of modesty. Even though his masterpiece has stalled, the inventor now believes that eventually he will succeed with another great idea. Such a belief helps the inventor stick to his guns and end up a persistent, self-sacrificing, hard worker whose creative juices never dried up with age.

It is often said of such individuals as Tolstoy, Verdi, and Titian, whose creativity continued throughout their exceptionally long lives, that their imaginations outlived their bodies. Certainly they did not burn out in middle age, as happens to so many promising young minds. Ironically, it is between the late thirties and early forties that the inventive stage makes a strong comeback. When it does return, you can count on the same things you experienced during the first appearance of the inventor:

Logic: The mind develops a tight, rational view of life.

Will power: The inventor is a persistent hard worker.

Sacrifice: He is flexible, accommodating, and willing to bend over backward to achieve a goal.

Public vs. private orientation: He is outgoing when he needs advice, but returns to his private world to weigh the pros and cons of this advice.

Crisis of long vs. short creative life: If the inventor receives backing and support, his creativity will continue throughout life.

1

The
Santa Claus
Scare

OBJECTIVE:
UNDERSTANDING
MYTHICAL
FIGURES

Is there really a Santa Claus? Adults have fielded this queston more often than any other on record. Of course there's a Santa. Talk to any merchant during the month of December if you need convincing. Better yet, buttonhole any six-year-old child. After that age, children leave home and may fall under the spell of some hard-nosed, worldly-wise classmates. Although these smart alecks are everywhere, they seem to abound in nursery schools on university campuses. Many are the offspring of learned professors and, as such, have traveled the globe on expeditions and research grants. Yet in their entire repertoire of speech, there's rarely an instance of "please," "thank you," "may I," "Sir or Ma'am." We call them "cultured barbarians." Poor Christopher suffered them one year when I was a graduate student. They did more to tarnish his image of Santa Claus than anything we had ever encountered. Cold, rational, and calculating, they waged a veritable crusade against old St. Nick. However, Christopher eventually beat these little brats at their own game.

Being of the twenty-first century, these intellectual snobs put little stock in folklore, yet could be sold the Brooklyn Bridge if the pitch were made over television. They were prodigies of the electronics age; TV transistors and cassette recorders were their bible. That was to be their downfall, as you shall see.

For years we had made tape recordings of Santa's visit to our home. With time, the production became fairly elaborate, almost rivaling the best of radio during its golden era. Mary provided the sound effects, bells and the sound of boots and reindeer hooves, while I provided the "ho, ho, ho." After a few dry runs, the tape rolled. Up I marched to the children's rooms, mentioning some personal highlight of the year, ticking off their gifts, and then planting "the magic kiss" on each forehead, which, with the help of Mary's special audio effects, sounded like a popping champagne cork.

On Christmas morning, the children would bail out of their beds and head to the tree like assault troops hitting the beach. After a few frantic minutes of tearing open presents, they would inevitably start begging for the Santa Claus tape. The tape became so famous that eventually every child in our neighborhood came around to get an earful of Santa.

Such an outpouring of interest and belief gave Christopher all the courage he needed. On the first day after the Christmas vacation, he brought the tape to school. You didn't need a crystal ball to predict the results: Most of the children were immediately convinced, a few were borderline, while one or two remained doubting Thomases. What grown-ups fail to understand is that a belief in Santa Claus and other great heroic figures is as much a part of the child's natural development as learning to talk, walk, read, or ride a bike.

Like developments in other areas, the belief in Santa goes through stages. At first, this belief is based solely on blind obedience to authority, namely, the parents' statement about whether there is or is not a Santa Claus. Next, the child hopes that by believing in Santa he'll get his presents. It's the old saw: You scratch my back, I'll scratch yours. The third level finds the youngster on the fence. He is in doubt, but continues to believe to please his parents or to keep peace in the house with his younger brothers or sisters. At the next stage, the child makes the break with belief not because of any hard reason but rather because he's going along with the crowd: in short, peer pressure. Finally, logical inconsistencies blow the belief to pieces: "How does he get all those toys for everyone in the world in one sleigh?"

Ask your youngster about Santa and use these stages to help gain some insight into his belief. Remember this belief passes through five stages: (1) blind obedience; (2) hope; (3) doubt; (4) peer pressure; and (5) logic.

DIARY:

2

Correspondence

OBJECTIVE:
HELPING THE CHILD SEE
ONE-TO-ONE
RELATIONSHIPS

Matty, one of Erin's best little pals, was down in the dumps because his father would be out of town on Christmas. But Erin had something up her sleeve to save the day. Erin knew that Matty had been eyeing one of Christopher's favorite toy soldiers for weeks, and she was going to put the touch on her brother.

Christopher was a softy, which put him in a terrible fix. How could he say no to Matty, yet how could he part with a favorite toy?

Our boy was in a real spot when Erin asked, "Can Matty have one of your army men? He doesn't have a father on Christmas." In a flash of genius Chris responded, "Then why don't we give him Daddy?"

Though some of the stuffing was knocked out of my ego, all was not lost. Christopher's solution did show that he had acquired the concept of *correspondence*. He was now able to make matches between different objects of various sizes: in effect, I was equal to one toy soldier. Earlier, as a poet, he would never have seen the connection. But now as an inventor, he understood the idea of correspondence: a unit of one item (a daddy) is equal to one unit of another item (a toy). If Matty had wanted two soldiers, then Christopher would have had to throw his mother into the deal to keep the correspondence equal, to make it a two-to-two relationship.

To see if your inventor has grasped the idea or correspondence, give her twenty buttons and the same number of straws. Spread out five buttons and ask her to place a straw under each one. Can she do it? Do bigger buttons get more than one straw? Next try it with ten, fifteen, and finally with twenty buttons.

DIARY:

3

Classification

OBJECTIVE:
RECOGNIZING THE
INVENTOR'S ABILITY
TO CATEGORIZE

Erik hadn't been at his grandmother's house for more than five minutes before he was hanging over the backyard fence trying to size up the kid next door. As the ritual goes, the two were soon locking horns in a duel of one-upmanship. Each made an effort to outdo the boast of the other. As inventors, they were obliged to stay within the boundaries of truth. It was tit for tat until Erik lowered the boom with, "My grandpa's an Eagle, Moose, Lion, and Elk," to which his flabbergasted adversary replied, "How much does it cost to see him?"

Aside from winning him a new friend, Erik's remark demonstrated that he had picked up the ability to classify, or pigeonhole, information into different categories. Among other uses, such a skill enables one to argue logically, which Erik's remark also demonstrated. Classification is a sure sign of inventive thinking. Armed with this new ability, the youngster is less likely to lie in order to get his way or make a point. Now he can reorganize facts rather than bend or deny them, as the poet was prone to do. For the poet, facts are something to be skirted when necessary, while the inventor is compelled to conform to reality and work with the facts.

Use the following activity to see if your child can classify: Cut out six circles, squares, and triangles from paper of different colors. Ask your child to stack them into groups that go together. Does he do it by size, color, or shape? Can he classify by all three of these qualities or is he stuck with one? The more a category system can be shifted, the better the inventor's understanding of classification.

DIARY:

4

Noah's
Ark

OBJECTIVE:
UNDERSTANDING THE
CHILD'S CONCEPT
OF LENGTH

Our children collected stray pets the way some kids collect bubble gum cards. At one time or another, we sheltered every type of domesticated animal imaginable, not to mention some unimaginable types, such as my cousin's boa constrictor who grew rather attached to my right arm.

It was generally at the end of the school year that our house ran second only to Noah's Ark..Every June teachers are prone to dump their menageries on willing pupils and unsuspecting parents. Fortunately for us, this year's catch was light: only two gerbils. Still, we paid dearly. With so few pets, the kids had lots of time on their hands, which led to a number of problems, the most interesting of which was how to tell the difference between these two gerbils. Everyone contributed advice. Mine was, "Why don't you name them?" This suggestion stood for a second before being rejected by Erik, who said, "They don't understand our talk." Erin piped up, "Why not shave one?" "That's too hard," replied Christopher, "but I have a good idea. Let's measure them." A vote wasn't even needed. The jury was in. Christopher's plan got the green light.

Erik quickly jumped into action by pinning one of the gerbils in the corner of its cage. At the same corner on the outside of the cage, the children placed a tape measure, which Erik pulled out until it was even with the tip of the gerbil's nose. It measured three inches. Sensing a similar fate, the second creature hightailed it out of his corner and was halfway across the cage before Erin nailed him in his tracks with her vicelike grip. Though no part of this gerbil was in the corner, Erik nonetheless again started measuring from the corner. Obviously this estimate of length was totally inaccurate. The kids had no idea of the concept of measurement. No one considered the fact that the second gerbil wasn't in the corner. What is important to the young inventor is the finishing line or the end of the object to be measured, not its starting point.

Does your inventor understand the concept of measurement? To find out, give her two soda straws of the same length. Lay the straws down parallel but move one an inch forward. Then ask the child which straw is the longest.

DIARY:

5

UFOs

OBJECTIVE:
RECOGNIZING STAGES
IN THE UNDERSTANDING
OF LANGUAGE

Nowadays you can't flip through the paper or switch on the news without encountering another UFO sighting, if not a landing.

To settle the question of little green men once and for all, I turned to our resident space cadet and put it right on the line, "Erin, are there such things as flying saucers?" Without a blink she snapped, "You bet. They have names, don't they?" Her response told us less about space visitors than it did about her notions of language. She was at a point in life where if something has a name, it exists. The name of an object and the object are one and the same. They naturally go together, like the association between the thought of a gelatin dessert and the thought of Jello. Once Christopher mentioned that he was going to bring home a friend named Peter. When Erin saw the friend, she cried, "He's not the rabbit!" As far as Erin was concerned, an object owns its name in the same way a title to a parcel of land shows that the holder has exclusive right to that property. The name *Peter* couldn't belong to anything but a rabbit.

Erin had a long way to go before she understood how language worked. The first breakthrough came when she realized that language originated from the speaker. Once she commented about a neighbor's baby, "He's got teeth, but his words haven't come in yet." This remark proved that she now saw language as something personal and subjective; it was no longer external, as it had been in the case of "Peter" the rabbit.

Finally she even pinpointed the location of language. It now seemed to stem from the head and was associated with thought. This new understanding came out loud and clear during a debate she was having with Christopher about the intelligence of different animals. He: "Parrots are smarter than dogs; these birds can talk." She: "But they can't think like dogs!" He: "Why?" She: "Because dogs have ears and birds don't."

Erin was equating thinking with the silent act of listening, which can only occur if one has ears. For her, "Thinking is the little voice that goes off in my head." In other words, thinking is internal speech. This notion of internal speech is far more advanced than Erin's earlier belief that language is associated with having teeth.

It's easy to see from Erin's experience that children pass through three stages in their understanding of language:

1. In the first stage, the child sees language as a collection of external labels, as in the case of "Peter" the rabbit. The child believes that others have made the labels that she has learned.

2. The child sees language as personal, being made by the individual and coming from the mouth.
3. The child's understanding is the same as in the second stage, except that she now sees language as being produced in the mind.

At what stage is your inventor operating? To find out, show her a picture of an animal, for example, an elephant. Then ask the following questions:

1. What is this animal called?
2. Where did it get its name?
3. How do we know that this is the animal's real name?
4. Why is this animal called an elephant?
5. Your name is Erin (substitute your child's name) and your friend's is Amy (substitute friend's name). Could you ever be called Amy and your friend Erin?

Questions 1 through 3 will give you some information about the first stage of understanding language, while questions 4 and 5 will provide insights about the second and third stages, respectively.

DIARY:

6

Conservation

OBJECTIVE:
UNDERSTANDING
VOLUME

In our neck of the woods, the first signs of spring were not flowers or robins, but the coming of the circus. As a kickoff to this spectacular event, our town put on an annual parade featuring clowns, tumblers, strong men, caged animals, cowboys and Indians, plus an assortment of pachyderms. One year, as an Indian brave in full war paint trotted past on his mount, Erin blurted, "Hey, Chief, you can't drive that horse, he just let out all his gasoline in a puddle." Embarrassed, I whispered, "That's not gas!"

"I know, I know,"she answered. Then, almost as an afterthought, Erin murmured, "Still, what a big puddle; it could've filled a jar."

Though the "gasoline" was never mentioned again, Erin wouldn't drop the idea of the puddle. As a matter of fact, puddles, sinks, rusty cans, or anything that held water became her number-one item of business during the next few days. It seemed from dawn to dusk she did nothing but empty water in and out of various containers. Through it all, she never tired of seeing how the same amount of water could be poured first into a long flat baking pan and then back into a tall watering can without there being a drop of water left over in the pan.

What all this play led to was the discovery of *conservation*, which represents a major breakthrough in the logical development of the inventor. With this discovery, the youngster is no longer fooled by the shape of containers. If you fill a tall skinny glass brimful with milk and then pour all that milk into a deep cereal bowl up to its brim, a child without an understanding of conservation will look at the bowl and say there's more milk in it than there was in the glass. This child is sidetracked by appearances. She has not yet grasped the idea of volume.

To see if your young inventor has developed an understanding of conservation, give her an eight-ounce cereal bowl and a tall eight-ounce glass filled with chocolate milk. Pour the milk into the bowl until the glass is empty. Then ask her if there was more milk in the glass than is in the bowl.

DIARY:

7

Five
Little
Bears

OBJECTIVE:
RECOGNIZING
SERIATION

One hobby we all enjoyed as a family was backpacking. As newcomers to the sport, most of our gear was an assortment of odds and ends and hand-me-downs. This was obvious when we ate; everyone's plate was scratched, chipped, and differed not only in color but in size as well.

As usual, Christopher made the best of the situation. He suggested that Papa Bear get the biggest plate and so on down the line with baby Erin receiving the smallest plate. His version of the three bears turned an otherwise boring task of setting the table into an entertaining fantasy. Each child begged to play Goldilocks so he or she could set out all the plates for the five Lehane bears. For Christopher, setting the table was a snap. Even blindfolded he could have dealt out the plates in a declining order that corresponded to each of our heights. Erin, being the youngest, treated the whole thing as a joke. She was merely having fun playing Goldilocks. But Erik had a problem. He couldn't get the hang of how to set the plates in order. Certainly he had no trouble in getting the biggest and smallest plates in their right positions; it was the remaining three plates, the in-between sizes, that really threw him.

Unlike Christopher, Erik had not reached the stage at which the concept of seriation is obtained. *Seriation* is the basic understanding of how to arrange objects by size. It is the basis of mathematical thinking.

Can your youngster seriate? This activity will help answer the question: Give the child five straws. Cut them so that they look like steps, with each straw being a quarter of an inch shorter than the one before it. Mix the straws up and ask the youngster to put them in order, starting with the tallest and ending with the shortest.

DIARY: _____

8

Grandpa's
Speeding Ticket

OBJECTIVE:
UNDERSTANDING THE
CHILD'S CONCEPT
OF SPEED

At times one of the best gifts you can give yourself is a little vacation away from the kids. A week seems to be good medicine for everyone's nerves. During this time span, the kids can't get too spoiled, and their grandparents, who usually graciously offer to fill in for us, don't quite reach the end of their rope. And as we all know, "absence makes the heart grow fonder," at least so the saying goes.

After being away for a week, our first greeting was a chorus of three soreheads moaning, "Why don't you come back tomorrow? Grandpa's going to jail and we won't be able to go with him now!" Perhaps Gramps had indeed reached the end of his rope. However, a more plausible explanation was forthcoming. It seems Gramps had gotten tagged for speeding and was off to appeal the charge. Christopher had already prepared his grandfather's defense: The speed of the car wasn't determined by Gramps' heavy foot, but by the tank having just been filled with gas. As far as Chris was concerned, it was an open-and-shut case. The more gas you had in the car, the faster it went. For Chris, there was no getting around it: A full tank was equal to full speed ahead.

Though Christopher's advocacy of his grandfather's case might have found a soft place in the judge's heart, his grasp of physics clearly represented nothing but soft and mushy thinking. Like most youngsters at the beginning of the inventor stage, Christopher had very little understanding of the concept of speed.

You can get an idea of how well children understand the concept of speed by drawing a target on a sheet of newspaper. Place a little racing car on the outside ring and another one on the inside ring. Ask the youngster the following question: If both cars raced around their tracks and finished at the same time, which one went faster? The young inventor won't realize that the car on the outside track had to cover more distance and so had to be traveling at a higher speed.

DIARY:

9

Go Fly
a Cloud

OBJECTIVE:
RECOGNIZING STAGES
IN THE UNDERSTANDING
OF PHYSICAL CAUSATION

It's hard to place a value on education. But after I had spent a couple of hundred dollars on a new set of encyclopedias, I found myself rapidly becoming educationally "trigger-happy." At the faintest request for information, I would shoot from the hip, as I did when Erik asked, "Can you fly a cloud?" Before he could take another breath, I had drawn my Britannica and was blasting away about wind currents and air pressure, only to succeed in completely killing Erik's interest in clouds.

Rather than being so quick to drum my boy's head full of adult facts, I should have realized one thing immediately: This was a kid's question and so only a kid's answer would do. It would have been far more appropriate to answer, "You don't fly clouds. They move by themselves to get away from the hot sun." Such a reply would have been in step with an inventor's ideas about physical motion. Obviously the inventor's ideas change: (1) At first, he believes that all objects move by themselves; thus a cloud walks away from the hot sun. (2) Next, there's the view that outside powers move objects. Flying a cloud and a kite are the same thing. Both can be pulled by a string in your hand. (3) Finally, there's the logical understanding that only a few objects, mainly people and animals, move on their own.

Which of these three beliefs makes sense to your child? To understand your child's ideas about physical causation, try the following questions. I've provided some answers that you can use as guides in evaluating the answers you receive.

Where do clouds come from? "From smoke."

What are clouds made of? "Stone."

Are clouds alive? "Yes." Why? "They can move."

How do they move? "By themselves." "The wind." "Thunder." "God."

What are clouds for? "Storms." "Lightning."

How does rain come from clouds? "When the clouds hit each other, pieces break off and fall as rain."

How do clouds make thunder? "They're stone and when they bump together, they crack and make a bad noise."

DIARY:

10

Snoring
to Death

OBJECTIVE:
RECOGNIZING THE
CHILD'S LEVEL
OF ARTIFICIALISM

The most effective form of birth control ever invented by Mother Nature can be found in most homes. It usually slips into your bed around two or three in the morning to remain lodged there like the Rock of Gibraltar between you and your spouse until the first crack of dawn. At that hour, it would greet me with, "Hi, Daddy. It's Erik."

Believe me, there's no moving a five-year-old once he has nestled cocoonlike under your covers. It's like trying to move forty pounds of deadweight. Only with a dirty trick like snoring in his ear was it possible to break Erik of this habit.

Yet, as luck would have it, the snoring never fazed Erin, who had immediately slid in to fill the opening left by her brother. Although my snorting and snoring would have put Ferdinand the Bull to shame, Erin refused to budge. Her only reaction was to count on her fingers. The louder I snored, the faster she counted. This had a snowballing effect. We were like two racehorses being driven down the backstretch neck and neck. God knows, we would've killed each other had we not both started to hyperventilate. I yelled, "Are you trying to kill us?" "No," she cried, "I'm trying to save you." As it turned out, Erin believed that I would die between snores if she didn't count to eight before my next snore. Crazy idea? Not if you're an inventor. The inventor still believes in *artificialism*—that is, that there is some purpose or plan behind everything. At first the master planner is God. He is the inventor's key to everything: "God made the stars, rivers, mountains, planets," and so on. Before long the inventor extends this divine power to great heroic figures, such as Paul Bunyan, Jack Frost, Santa Claus, the tooth fairy, and the man in the moon, as well as to some unsavory figures, such as the devil, ghosts, Wolfman, and other monsters. The inventor includes parents with these heroes and antiheroes. We too are assumed to have superpowers. Once when I was disappointed because our picnic had been rained out, Erin was astonished because she felt I had the power to control the rain simply by phoning the weatherman.

As these ideas begin to fade, they are replaced by a new view that holds that the world can be understood, if not controlled, by reciting magical formulas: counting to eight, chanting "rain, rain go away" or "one potato, two potato," and so on. Since none of these formulas give him the immediate results he wanted, the inventor eventually feels cheated. He is now ready to kiss artificialism good-bye. At this stage if asked, why the sky is blue, he'll fumble around for words, in effect saying, "It's hard to know." With this, the inventor is taking the first step toward looking for the natural causes of things.

Try to pinpoint your inventor's level of artificialism by asking why the moon changes shapes; why it's not always round; and why it gets smaller. Here are some possible answers:

"God makes the moon change so we know what day it is."

"The man in the moon is worn out from all his work of shining."

"Pieces of the moon fall to the ground and make rain."

"When I say my prayers, the moon goes to bed too."

DIARY:

11

Reversibility

OBJECTIVE:
ANALYZING AN
IMPORTANT LOGICAL
DEVELOPMENT

Kids have their own pet theories of change. Erik even had one about human cycles. He believed that as adults grow older they shrink. It never crossed his mind that it was his own growth that was closing the gap between us.

Though this notion was off base, it did show some indication that Erik was becoming more logical. Earlier he had believed that as soon as an object altered its size or shape, it became something new. However, he was now able to see that things can look different but remain the same, that a change in appearances doesn't always mean a change in the basic nature of an object. (In this instance, I was still Daddy even though I appeared to be getting smaller or shrinking.)

This type of reasoning is called *reversibility*, which means the ability to perceive that although certain parts of an object have been switched around, the object nonetheless remains the same. For example, you can break the number 5 into many combinations, 4 and 1, 3 and 2, 5 and 0, all of which still add up to 5.

Has your inventor developed reversibility? Here's how to find out. Give your child two indentical balls of clay, placing one in each of his hands. Ask him if they weigh the same. Next, roll one of the balls into a hot dog. Now ask if the two clay objects weigh the same. A yes answer indicates that your child can reverse.

DIARY:

12

No Dessert

OBJECTIVE:
UNDERSTANDING THE
CHILD'S CONCEPT
OF JUSTICE

Every once in a while, especially after trying on a pair of pants that once fit like a glove but are now too snug, I go on a calorie kick and start rearranging our daily menu until it resembles something that only a rabbit could live with: raw carrots, lettuce, spinach, and so on.

As you can imagine, the Lehane kids usually turn up their noses at such fare, which leaves me at a crossroads: Do I order them to stay at the table until their plates are clean? Or do I come up with a clever little trick to make it easier? Unfortunately, there are nights on which no decision is involved. I simply lose all patience and growl, "Eat your greens or else...." On one such night Erin held her ground and refused to nibble a morsel. I was so furious over her stand that I barked, "OK, that means no dessert for you." Wincing, she retorted, "That's not fair. I'll go to my room for the night. But don't take my dessert." What a twisted view of justice, I thought. Her own punishment is harsher than mine. But then it hit me. A young child's sense of fair play stems from a belief in *retributive justice*—that is, punishment is seen as something like medicine; it tastes awful and hurts, but it's something *you have to take*. However, this idea makes no allowances for something that may be *taken away from you*, such as dessert. The child fails to appreciate the logic that if she doesn't eat one type of food, another type should be taken away. This type of punishment is based on *distributive justice*; it tries to set up an equal situation or logical one. Most of the "logical" punishments adults hand out are seen by kids as inappropriate, hence funny.

> *Equal situation:* Erin loses Christopher's yo-yo and so has to give him hers. She thinks this is cruel.

> *Logical Situation:* While jumping around, Erin breaks one of the slats in her bed and so has to sleep in this bed, which slumps down. Erin considers this fun; she doesn't understand it as a punishment.

To gauge how your child views justice, tell her the stories of the yo-yo and the broken bed slat and ask her how the child should be punished.

DIARY:

13

"I Didn't Mean It"

OBJECTIVE:
UNDERSTANDING
THE CHILD'S
MORALITY CODE

A few years ago a special report was issued on a car that was extremely hazardous to drive. The report was called "Dangerous at Any Speed," and that, in a nutshell, described our Erik.

Whereas most kids run and jump when excited, our boy launched himself like a guided missile, only in this case the missile was unguided. Neither he nor anyone else had any idea of where he'd land once launched, except that it was bound to be on top of something very expensive and fragile. Any house he stepped into unfailingly suffered some accidental breakage. It got so bad that we kept him out of stores, which did little for his self-confidence. We told him a hundred times that these were all accidents, that he hadn't done it on purpose.

Nonetheless, from Erik's point of view, he was morally responsible, if not guilty, for all the damage he caused. One morning when I was late for work and gobbling down my eggs, Erik reached across the table and accidentally spilled his orange juice on my trousers. In his rush to help me, he shook the table with such force that it sent a tidal wave of oatmeal over my shirt and favorite tie. I proceeded to give him a real dressing down despite his pleas, "I didn't mean it. I didn't mean it." To these I callously snapped, "Don't give me that! Go to your room!"

You don't have to be a mind reader to know the confusion that was going on in Erik's head. Erik was at a stage in life where he judged his actions solely by their consequences. Breaking twelve cups, even by accident, was worse than breaking three out of revenge. In the young child's moral code, it is numbers, not motives, that count. In this light, it's easy to see why Erik thought so little of himself.

To bolster his self-image, we had spent weeks before that morning when I was late for work drumming into him the idea that motives are more important than consequences. Then just as the idea looked as if it were going to sink in, all our work was suddenly washed away by a single glass of orange juice. "Last week I broke *twelve* cups and Daddy said it was okay because I didn't mean to. Now I spill *one* glass of juice that I didn't mean to and I'm in trouble up to my neck."

Erik was right. We had given him one set of instructions, but when we suffered because of his actions, we discarded those instructions. With our inconsistency, we were throwing curves at Erik, which, among other things, caused a relapse in his moral development. He was now back to thinking of consequences rather than motives.

To see where your child stands on moral issues, tell him a story about a youngster who, upon coming home for lunch, accidentally swings open the kitchen door so hard that the big glass pane in the door is shattered. Is the youngster to blame? Is he right or wrong (good or bad)? Why? Next see how your child reacts to a story of another youngster who is so mad at his mother that he tears a small page in her favorite book. Did your child judge the youngster by his motives or by the size of the damaged he caused (a big pane of broken glass versus a small torn page)?

DIARY:
_____

14

Daredevils
and Brats

OBJECTIVE:
UNDERSTANDING THE
THE CHILD'S DISPLAY OF
HIS SELF-IMAGE

One summer we rented a place in the mountains sight unseen. To say the least we were all a bit worried about what to expect. But even our worst nightmares couldn't have softened the blow. Though the cabin was situated among tall trees with plenty of fresh air, no one had thought to mention that it was perched on the edge of what looked like the Grand Canyon. However, the perilousness of its location dimmed in comparison to the road one had to take to reach it. The road was so high and full of curves that it was best described as "dead man's drive."

It was absolutely taboo for any of the children to play anywhere near the road, let alone on it. So you can imagine my horror one morning when I saw Christopher zooming down the drive on his bike going so fast that he was a mere blur. In the split second it took him to whizz down the mountain, I turned gray, dropped two pant sizes, and almost choked on my heart. Fortunately he walked away from this ordeal without a scratch, but he still had to deal with me. Before I could corner him, he blurted out, "Erik double-dared me."

No self-respecting five-year-old backs down from a double dare, especially one hurled by a pip-squeak of a brother. Christopher's manhood was on the line, at least so he thought. This was a particular tender issue for our little lad who had just weathered a fretful period of trying to piece together his self-image.

In taking up Erik's challenge, Christopher ran the risk not only of getting hurt but of catching my wrath as well. But these risks were nothing when you remember that Christopher saved himself from being called a chicken or, worse, from being emotionally crushed or humiliated.

This is not the time for a grown-up to start preaching about inner convictions or sticking to one's guns when others taunt and tease. The child's pride and honor are at stake. By all means, warn him of the physical dangers; in fact, draw them out in gory detail. But then give him an honorable out. Have him come up with his own double dares that are relatively safe—for example, walking in the dark or picking up worms.

Cannonballing down a driveway isn't the only way that children display images of themselves to the world: some turn bold and bratty, while others begin to brag. A youngster who always goes around blowing his own horn usually has a pretty shaky image of himself. Such a big mouth can turn very bashful and mousy if others see through his boasting and laugh at him. On the other hand, the bold, sassy brat is generally overly pampered; he thinks he's great and won't rest until everyone else thinks the same way. Then there are a handful of children who, when their ego ideals are challenged, react in less obvious, if not more constructive and imaginative, ways: clowning around, racing one another, strutting, prancing, and even in speaking—for instance, calling their parents by their first names, "Hi, Mary. Hi, Steve."

All these behaviors boil down to one thing: various ways of showing off one's self-image. How many ways does your child have? Does he boast, or is he bashful? How does he handle double dares? Does he come up with his own challenges? Does he ever show off in his speech (an affected accent, name dropping, and so forth)?

DIARY:

15

Slick
Tricks

OBJECTIVE:
RECOGNIZING THE
STRATEGIES AND EXCUSES
OF THE INVENTOR

Christopher had a new angle for getting himself out of jams: slick tricks. While being chewed out, he would usually pass a perceptive comment, such as, "Dad, when you get steamed up and mad at me, you talk without moving your jaw." Without fail, such remarks caused me to snicker, if not to roar with laughter, thereby breaking the tension between us and getting Christopher off the hook. The lad had developed a perfect sense of timing and a flawless delivery.

Our boy's new "slipperiness," which got him out of tight squeezes, was a far cry from his earlier blunt temper tantrums. Instead of those awful power plays and outbursts, which brought him nothing but more trouble, he had now created an entire system of evasive actions for saving his hide and slipping out of obligations. Here is a list of some of these evasive actions:

SPLITTING HAIRS
Teacher: "Don't ever let me catch you pulling the cat's tail again!" Chris: "I wasn't pulling it; I was just holding it hard."

PLAYING UP TO YOU
Knowing his mother was an avid naturalist, Chris would say, "Mom, I can't come for dinner now. I'm chasing a butterfly."

PLAYING DEAF AND DUMB
"I'm sorry"; "I didn't know that"; or "What did you say?"

ACTING THE MARTYR:
On seeing his daddy eat dessert, Christopher might say, "I'm not going to ask anyone for cake," or, "I hope someone offers me something to eat."

SCAPEGOATING:
After breaking a cup, he might state, "It wasn't strong. It was cheap. Someone put it in front of me."

USING LOGIC:
Being told that his sister always ate everything off her plate, he would counter, "Yes, but God made Erin and me different."

Keep in mind that these techniques represent a pretty inventive intelligence. The youngster is trying to play your game, to deal with you on a reasonable and verbal plane, rather than knocking heads with you, as he did in his earlier and more primitive temper tantrums.

At this stage, kids' ways of sidestepping responsibilities and getting out of hot water can be uncanny. Does you child use any of the actions listed above? Mention a few to him and ask if he's ever used them. What are his favorite techniques? Which ones irritate you? Which ones work with different people? (Grandmothers and aunts are suckers for most of these techniques.) Have you observed other tricks not included in this list?

DIARY:

16

"Cross My Heart"

OBJECTIVE:
USING VERBAL CONTRACTS
OR OATHS TO
SETTLE DISPUTES

I could have retired years ago if I had a dollar for every time one of my children moaned, "It's my toy. I had it first," and another retorted, "No, it isn't. It's mine." I don't know how you handle such disputes, but in a recent one between Erik and Erin, our little girl came up with something ingenious. She dragged out a big Sears catalogue and, with her right hand raised, shouted, "Honest to

God, cross my heart and hope to die, I would never tell a lie. It's my toy."

Erin had lifted a page right out of a "Perry Mason" script. Mimicking a witness, she was establishing truth by swearing on a makeshift bible. Far from being a mere act of imitation, Erin's actions showed that she now understood that if one follows certain rituals, one's word or opinion then becomes as good as gold. This is a true sign of inventive thinking.

When younger, Erin had felt that honor, or for that matter, any moral issue could be settled solely by her own word, "The toy's mine. I said so." Now she had come to grips with the notion that morality hinges not so much on one's own word as it does on uttering special socially acceptable formulas, such as swearing on a Bible. At this stage of development, the inventor has a whole network of special oaths and formulas to cover most of her dealings:

SEALING A CONTRACT
Erin: "What goes up a chimney?"
Erik: "Smoke."
Erin: "This bargain never broke."

Chris: "What's this?"
Erik: "A brick."
Chris: "Your promise will always stick."

Erin: "If I don't do it, I'll eat a worm" or "you can have my pencil."
Whenever a child is willing to endure something hateful, like eating a worm or suffering the loss of something special, it's a good bet she's on the up-and-up.

OFFERING EVIDENCE:
"I have new boots. Hear them squeak."

Erik: "A fly (bee) burned me with his foot."
Chris: "Flies don't have fire in their feet."
Erik: "Oh, yeah, put your finger on one and see!"

APPEALING TO A JUDGE OR JURY:
The youngster goes to parents, teacher, or older kids for backing for her opinions.

RECITING OATHS:
> These oaths consist of special phrases, such as "honest to God," "cross my heart," and so on.

The use of these special formulas points to two developments in the inventor's life. First, she is breaking out of her shell and becoming more social. Because of this, she relies more on the standards or codes that others her age use to guide their behavior. Second, as a result of her growing sociability, the youngster is a little unsure of herself, a little psychologically shaky, and so has a need for the moral crutches that the oaths and rituals provide.

If you should encounter a serious dispute among children, here's an activity for getting at the root of the problem: Take each child to a private area, such as a closet or a big box that's used only for this purpose. Then ask her what happened. Next have her recite one of the oaths. If there's no reprisal for what the child reveals and if this ritual of being taken to the private area is used only when the dispute involves very high stakes, then in most cases you will get as honest an account as you can expect from an inventor.

DIARY:

17

Bed
Womb

OBJECTIVE:
UNDERSTANDING THE
CHILD'S DEFINITION
OF SEX ROLES

If you want to gain some insight into your inventor's understanding of sex, take him for a family swim at your local YMCA. On our first visit Erik peeked into the locker room where he spied a bunch of grown-ups changing to go swimming. He then told Christopher, who asked, "Are they men or girls?" Erik looked again and then answered, "I can't tell; they don't have clothes on."

I know it's hard to believe, but for young children, the distinguishing marks of gender are hairstyle and dress, not body parts. Discussion of the functions of a penis, vagina, and so on, has little meaning for them. In telling Christopher that his mother was pregnant, I explained how the baby was living in her womb. He then went to nursery school and commenced to fill his teacher in on his mother's condition: "My mommy's having a baby and I know where she's keeping it." "Where?" asked his teacher. "In the living womb, where else?" Despite my detailed explanation, Christopher's young mind had translated *womb* to *room*.

Having been burnt once, I was hesitant about using such clinical terms with my other two kids. That's why when Erin saw me step out of the shower and asked, "What's that?" I didn't say "penis." Instead, I told her that that's what makes me a daddy. Later that day I overheard her talking to some of her girl friends: "Do you have a daddy [i.e., a penis]? I don't."

No doubt sex education is a loaded and ticklish issue. But if we approach it as we do other concerns of children, we can handle it with some grace and ease. The basic rule is to supply the inventor only with information that fits his present level of thinking. Thus to the proverbial question "Who made me?" try answering "God." We used this answer satisfactorily for months until Erik finally asked, "But where did He get the parts?" Obviously the mystical belief that we're fashioned in heaven no longer sat right with Erik because he had now reached a stage of development where he figured that not even the Almighty could make something from nothing. Like us, God needed building parts or materials—like clay, dust, mud—anything would do. In effect, our boy was digging for a more down-to-earth explanation of his origins, which was finally supplied by the "seed theory" of birth. This theory correlates having a baby with growing a garden in that both processes start with a seed. However, the seed theory places little emphasis on how the seed is planted. What is important is to describe the seed as being about the size of a marble. Don't start lecturing about a tiny speck of a sperm that can only be seen by a high-powered microscope. Remember, for an inventor, seeing is believing. There is no way he's going to believe that a baby can grow out of something that's invisible to the naked eye.

When kids do start wondering about how the seed was planted, they themselves come up with the "doctor theory." According to this theory, a physician surgically removes the seed from daddy and then performs another operation to put the seed in mommy's tummy. Don't panic when you hear this theory and try to fill the inventor's head with details about intercourse. The very idea of such impregnation turns kids off. The only experience they can compare it with is getting "a needle in you," and that hurts. Youngsters eventually get to the nitty-gritty of asking about the role daddy played in their birth, and then is the appropriate time to introduce a few of the basic clinical terms.

Young children don't see the connection between genitalia and sexuality. Despite today's flip-flop fashions, with men sporting shoulder-length curls and earrings and women wearing short-cropped hair and pantsuits, children still use hairstyle and dress as the chief way of distinguishing between the sexes. Not until around age six or seven do they begin to equate different body parts with different sex roles.

To see how your inventor defines sex roles, cut out some magazine pictures that show only the backs of heads. When asked to pick out the male and female, does the youngster assign sex roles on the basis of the traditional short hair for men and long hair for women? Next show the child pictures of models wearing a variety of clothes but whose heads are not included in the pictures. Does the child always identify pants and ties with males and frilly shirts with females? Some ads show models who are bare-breasted. If you cut the ad so only the torso with the breast is shown, can the child identify the sex properly? Ask the child if it's easier to draw a picture of a boy and girl with or without clothes. Then ask why one is easier to draw than the other.

DIARY:

18

Favors

OBJECTIVE:
UNDERSTANDING
ALTRUISM

Christopher seemed to have a mental block about saying "thank you" to people in his family. Once when he was fished out of a stream by Erin, he didn't even whisper a thanks but was loud to complain that Erin had scratched him on the wrist during the rescue. Yet when a fair-weather friend split a mere piece of chewing gum with our boy, nothing could have prevented Christopher from returning the favor.

Was this simply a case of Christopher's liking his pal more than his sister? I don't think so. The exchange of gifts or favors between kids isn't so much a show of friendship as it is a show of power. When youngsters are on equal footing, as were Christopher and his pal, there's almost a legal obligation to repay the donor in kind, immediately at whatever the cost. This repayment amounts to upholding one's honor. However, being saved by a little kid sister does nothing for an older brother's sense of honor and strength. If anything, it makes him look weak. In our case, what made the matter worse was that Erin also saw it as a power play and never missed any occasion to rub it in: "Nanny, Nanny, I saved Chris last week." Under these conditions Christopher's only choice was to ignore the favor and strike out at the person trying to siphon off his power.

Eventually the child begins to recognize a favor as an act of kindness without any strings attached to it. The favor is a moral debt to be paid back sometime in the future, whenever the donor is in need. Thus children tend to look upon favors in three ways: (1) as a power play; (2) as a legal obligation; and (3) as a social commitment.

To see how your youngster views favors, try the following activity: Ask what his greatest wish is. Then ask him how he would treat the person who granted him that wish if that person were: one of his parents, his brother or sister, a female playmate, a male playmate, or his teacher. If the child feels that he would lose power by accepting the favor from that particular person he will describe his thanks in a flat tone, without much heart. Kids who are spoiled may just expect favors and so may not express any reaction; it would be lowering themselves too much. On the other hand if the child feels a legal obligation to respond or if he feels each favor has to be paid back with another, then you should hear one of the following: (1) "I'd share it with him"; (2) "I'll give him something he likes"; (3) "I'll give him my pooh bear that I love"; (4) "I'll think of something." Between the first and the fourth responses, there is a decreasing tendency to repay the donor with the exact favor or one high in value. In the last response, there is almost the awareness that "I'll be around if he needs me," which gets at the heart of true giving. The child is in effect saying that he has an obligation and will pay it off in whatever way best suits the donor at the time of the donor's need. This response involves a sense of cooperation and teamwork.

DIARY:

19

My Brother's Keeper

OBJECTIVE:
RECOGNIZING THE
REACTIONS OF
SIBLING RIVALRY

The " catalog of horrors" is what I call all those dirty tricks our kids used to play on each other. The dirtiest were always saved for the arrival of a family member; a prime example was the time Mary caught Christopher trying to stuff his new baby brother into a dresser drawer.

What we were seeing was the other side of brotherly love, sibling rivalry. Sibling rivalry is a natural condition that flares up when a child feels his brother or sister is getting too much attention; in short, it is jealousy. It really hits a peak with the birth of a new baby. As this newcomer occupies center stage, the older child fights back trying to regain his portion of it.

But it's not lack of attention alone that sets off sibling rivalry. There are other causes. Although we had promised Christopher a playmate, he found that all he got was a little squirt who slept all day. On top of this, Christopher's sense of security may have been suffering for when his mother was whisked away to the hospital to have Erik, Christopher must have thought she'd run out on him. I must have put the finishing touch on things by trying to pinch-hit for Mary: all I really managed to do was mess up our daily household routines and stir up confusion.

When you look at it this way, the arrival of a new baby doesn't seem exactly designed to promote the well-being of older siblings. They may suffer from insecurity, confusion, and a sense of deception, not to mention loneliness now that their parents' love is being drained off by this newcomer. It's no wonder kids strike out and rebel when a new baby arrives. However, some don't. These youngsters go around blaming themselves rather than the baby for all the trouble in their lives. They feel they must have failed their parents in some way; otherwise why would their parents have brought this strange creature home? When this happens, the older child tries to win back his parents by becoming an overachiever—that is, he tries to be perfect in every phase of life, even if that means becoming the best big brother a baby ever had.

Finally, there are a handful of youngsters who, after some early stress and strain, make an adjustment to the baby that most parents would consider normal. Their actions are similar to those of the overachievers except that overachievers down deep continue to hold a grudge against their younger siblings.

In sum, a child may react to a new baby in three ways: (1) by striking out; (2) by overachieving; and (3) by adjusting normally.

The last two reactions may entail similar behavior. To distinguish between these reactions, tell your child the following story, changing the sexes of the children to match your circumstances: While two brothers are playing, the younger one without permission borrows the older brother's favorite toy and breaks it by mistake. The overachiever who still has a streak of jealousy in him will show signs of wanting revenge on his younger brother as he answers these questions:

1. What should happen to the little brother?
   "He should be punished."
2. Even if he didn't do it on purpose?
   "Yes, because he didn't ask me."
3. What if the younger child just forgot to ask permission?
   "It doesn't matter, he still broke the toy."
4. What should happen to the little one?
   "He should be hit." (Pain is emphasized.)
5. What should the big brother get?
   "Any toy he wants" or "A chance to take and break the little boy's favorite toy."
6. Could the little boy pick out a toy to give to the bigger boy?
   "No, because he'd just give him an old toy."

DIARY:

20

Never
Say Die

OBJECTIVE:
UNDERSTANDING HOW
INVENTORS VIEW
DEATH

If you want to understand how kids view death, take them to see *Snow White*. Whether Disney knew it or not, his movie touches upon all the ideas that kids have about dying.

At first children think of death as nothing but a long sleep. Next they begin to weep because they realize that dying is a permanent separation from family and friends. To soften this blow, they invent the idea of heaven, reincarnation, or some other way of reuniting everyone after a long separation. Soon an idea even better than heaven pops up, and that is that if you can recognize death, you can avoid it. So death now takes on the image of the Grim Reaper or some other figure or symbol, be it a skull and bones, a hearse, or a cemetery. Eventually the child sees death as a penalty for doing something wrong.

In short, death for young children has many meanings: sleep; a sorrowful loss and separation from loved ones; heaven or a reunion; an image or symbol; and a penalty for having sinned.

Disney's production includes each one of these meanings. As the story goes, Snow White dies after disobeying (*sin*) the dwarfs by letting the ugly old lady (*image*) into their cottage, who then poisons (*penalty*) our heroine. Disney then vividly portrays *sorrow* and *loss* with the sobbing dwarfs, a raging rainstorm, and candles whose melting wax looks like tears. Interestingly, our heroine isn't buried in a coffin but placed on a bed (*sleep*) until Prince Charming's kiss awakens her (*reunion*).

Death may be hard for us to discuss , but kids find it fascinating because as we just noted, they feel they have a way of dealing with it. Here's an activity that may help you understand how young children view death: Ask the child what would happen to a bug that was stepped on and then died. Could the insect be awakened? If not, what happens to it? Would anybody be sorry? Do bugs have their own death? Does the bug's death look like anything or anyone? Do bugs die because they did something wrong? If you change the bug to a person the youngster knows, are there any differences in his answers to these questions? (With the actual loss of a loved one, the child may focus on the reunion aspect of death.)

DIARY:

21

Puppy Love

OBJECTIVE:
UNDERSTANDING
FEARS

Erin's first love stood a head taller than her nursery school teacher, tipped the scales at almost two hundred pounds, and packed away enough grub at dinner to feed an army. He was neither a pro football player nor a wrestler. He was in fact Ruppert Big Boy Jones, our St. Bernard, so docile and good-natured that he made "Gentle Ben" look rabid, and that's what made him so lovable.

Kids have a built-in fear of yapping little dogs who constantly dart around nipping at one's heels. The young child wants a pet to be a dependable, good old buddy—a copilot or imaginary friend who will fly along with the child on imaginative adventures. In short, the child is looking for a trusted companion, which rules out the high-strung and skittish gerbil, guinea pig, and even the cat as a good pet at this age. The problem is not so much that these animals will turn on one as that their actions are unpredictable. Their sudden movements, as well as their sharp cries or barks, are naturally feared by the child, as is anything that is unpredictable. What it all boils down to is that there are certain surprises kids can't live with.

Fear of the unpredictable is never lost. Like all the other fears of childhood, it is often so hard to live with that it is pushed down and hidden inside of us. Fears must be kept out in the open. If not, they can weigh the child down and turn him into an emotional cripple.

Keep in mind that fears do not decrease with age; they are merely pushed out of sight for a time but manage always to return to tangle up the child's life. The longer you can keep a child from hiding her fears, the easier it is to help her. Here are some steps for keeping fears aboveground: Don't hide your feelings; react openly when you're frightened. By seeing you cope with your problems, the child may learn how to deal with hers. (Some people argue that if you do as I suggest, the youngster may adopt the problem rather than its solution. However, the chances of this happening are very slim because most fears at this stage are natural, often stemming from unpredictable situations.)

One way to get at what's bothering the child is to tell her stories built around a childhood fear. One fear that touches the lives of many children is that of being left alone. Kids become so used to having their parents around that life becomes totally unpredictable when parents are absent. Such feelings are conveyed in *Peter Rabbit* and *Curious George.* When separated from their parents, the two main characters of these stories always get into a mess of trouble. Ask your child how Peter and George got into trouble. Was it their fault, or were their mothers to blame because they weren't there? How would the youngster handle such a situation? Using stories, help the child to bring both her imagination and reasoning to bear on the problem or fear.

Finally, try to anticipate those situations that trigger off fear in kids. Erin used to hate visiting her best friend because our little girl didn't know what to expect at her friend's house. You may have to accompany your child a few times so she can see firsthand what's going on.

DIARY:

CHAPTER

IV

CREATIVE ENVIRONMENTS

Ten seconds to blast off, nine, eight.... It's getting harder to swallow. Your heart's pounding. Yet racing through your mind as the final seconds tick off is a checklist: pencil box, Kleenex, lunch money. In the split second before Erik steps on the bus for his first day of school, the list flashes for the last time: crayons, bus pass, pants with pockets.

Pants with pockets? Believe me, they are as much a part of school as the three Rs. We learned this lesson the hard way last year with Christopher. As far as he was concerned, one day of school was enough; he had had his fill. On the next morning when I went to wake him, Chris looked startled and asked, "Why are you getting me up?" "For school," I answered. "What, again?" he replied. There was no way of breaking Christopher's grip on his bedpost that morning unless we swore we'd get him those pants by dinner time.

Pants with pockets aren't just picked off the racks at your local Sears, especially if your child's build is on the slim side of Don Knotts's. Christopher was so scrawny that on some days he had a hard time casting a shadow. Be that as it may, after rifling through all the toddler shops in town, we finally unearthed a pair for the measly sum of fifteen dollars. The price was more than worth it. Apparently pockets are a luxury for youngsters, a fact that had always escaped me until the night I was pulling off Chris's new duds, when from out of his pockets rolled three spit balls, some pebbles, half a squirrel's tail, a pencil with its eraser chewed off, not to mention a partially chewed crust from last week's jelly sandwich. The only clutter I'd ever seen to match this was the contents of Mary's purse. Kiddingly, I often told her some psychologist was going to make a million dollars by analyzng women's personalities on the basis of what they toted around in their handbags. However, in Christopher's case, the relationship between clutter and personality was not really farfetched. His pockets gave us a bird's-eye view of his private world. They also showed us how little of that world existed in school.

Classrooms are public arenas. One is always in the open and in public view. There's no place to hide or even to stash one's prized personal effects. No wonder then that pockets rate so high with children, as does the perennially favorite pastime of dropping blankets over desks to make tents. Pockets, tents, and cubbyholes act as hideouts in what otherwise seems like a fishbowl existence. Once in these private nooks, the child's creative machinery starts humming.

Schools play down privacy because they're in the business of fitting us into the public world. Unfortunately they do it at quite a cost; even one's most personal acts sooner or later fall under their strict control. In Christopher's class, for example, everyone had to learn to "pee" at half-past ten because that's the time his room had been slotted to use the lavatory. At home he was free to relieve himself at any time and in a variety of locations, his favorite being the peach tree on the side of our garage. With all our advanced and sophisticated know-how in child psychology, isn't it odd that the one standard that automatically bars a child from school has nothing to do with his intellect or personality, but with whether or not he's potty trained?

To be sure, schools merely mirror the larger public culture in which most of us participate: punching in at nine and out at five;

being sent out to pasture at age sixty-five; learning to read in the first grade whether you're up to it or not. Fortunately there are places where public time is all but stalled. Resorts in the Caribbean, Las Vegas, the French Quarter of New Orleans—all run on impulse rather than clocks. In point of fact, public clocks in these places are as scarce as hen's teeth. Just try to find one. Even the big digital signs of modern banks in these places display only temperature, not time. After the hustle and bustle of the first few days of vacation wear off, you suddenly find yourself lounging and relaxing more, if not being downright lazy. You're becoming a private person again. It's no wonder you come back from such carefree places supercharged with hope and new ideas. You've had the freedom to dream, which is the inspiration of all creativity.

One doesn't have to venture to these far-flung oases to capture privacy. In fact one need not go beyond one's own front door. As the saying goes, "a home is a man's castle." It shields him from the public world. Here he is king. This is even true for the child. No matter how large the family, there is always some place, some thing, or some person he can call his own. At home one eats when one's stomach growls, not just during those fifteen minutes set aside each school morning for snack. At home you paint till the urge dries up, not till quarter past two because after then Mrs. Jones's class is scheduled for the art room.

Unfortunately, the child who attends preschool at a very young age is robbed of much of the privacy he would otherwise be getting at home. As we stressed earlier, privacy is the source of creativity. Though one's ideas must be ultimately tested and proven in the public world, they get their start in our private worlds.

Interestingly, today more and more parents are choosing *family* day care (where a half-dozen or so kiddies are supervised in a friend's home under the watchful eye of the neighborhood's granny) rather than *institutional* day care (where a class of anywhere from twenty to fifty youngsters are supervised by certified teachers in the basement of a public school or in the wing of a plant). The choice of family over institutional care has in all probability little to do with the issue of creativity. It is more likely the result of the parents' sense for the chemistry that goes on in the more private settings. In comparing day-care youngsters with those who stayed at home, it has been found that the latter show both their good and bad feelings quite freely, while the day-care children seem to have built walls around their feelings. Their typical response to frustration is thumb sucking, whereas children cared for at home tend to walk away from bad situations in search of better ones.

Living in public and private settings clearly has a variety of effects upon children, the effect on creativity being just one. However, creativity deserves special attention because we are now attempting to substitute the privacy under which it has flourished with more public forms of child rearing, namely, day care, nursery school, and kindergarten. This is not a philosophical stand against early childhood schooling. If it were, I could drum up some provocative historical evidence that shows that whenever a country is in turmoil and the state seeks to restore order (i.e., to ensure that everyone thinks according to the party line), the state itself takes over the rearing of its citizens through day care. Russia, China, and Israel are examples, as was our own tentative effort to establish national day care during the politically turbulent 1960s. However, I'm not a foe of early childhood education; this is not my cause. I'm a specialist trained in the area and, quite frankly, I should be pushing day care. Yet I want to make sure we just don't blindly jump on the day-care bandwagon without realizing the problems that need to be worked out, the most obvious of which deals with creativity and the rearing of young children.

If they are to foster creativity, all early childhood facilities should be a blend of both the private and public, with those catering to the youngest child featuring the heaviest dosage of privacy. By privacy I mean a situation that affords ample opportunities for youngsters to spend time alone. Such a condition could exist in any setting from institutional to family day care. Ideally three-fourths of day care, one-half of nursery school, and one-fourth of kindergarten would be private.

In the pages that follow, suggestions will be given for making parts of the early school environment (its use of space, time, materials, and so on) more responsive to the creative needs of young children.

SPACE

Spend some time in the world of the five-year-old and you will find it inhabited by two types: boys and yuks. Yuks can't play with boys and, on long sweaty field trips, they never get to sit by the open bus window on the way back to school.

Obviously, I'm talking about girls and how they're put down by little boys. Sex discrimination is bad enough, but things really get out of hand when the school has a bully like Frank the Tank. On the surface Frank appears to be nothing more than a bossy little bore. But put him in the right situation, for example, recess, and Frank can show a mean streak a mile wide, chasing, taunting, and menacing every girl in sight.

Erin always stood up to him and, as could be expected, they fought like cats and dogs—except for the morning Frank and his henchmen were pretending an old refrigerator carton was a fort. Erin was playing with them. Her part? A big stone guarding the fort. For better or worse, the "big stone" broke the sex barrier. It seemed that the box had sparked imaginative play, and it soon also became clear that as the fantasy increased, the discrimination on all levels—sex, color, ability, and age—decreased. This experience was a real eye-opener and drove home the message of how powerful private spaces like boxes are in fostering creative behavior. To squeeze every ounce of imaginative play out of the box, it should be decorated like a billboard, suggesting a particular play topic, and should include props that fit the topic.

Just as boxes excite imagination, desks and chairs—the most common type of spacial setup in the classroom—hem it in. In terms of fostering creativity, open space—a wide area of the room usually marked off by a rug—is midway between boxes and desks. Being nothing but empty space it does very little in the way of guiding play, as do the boxes. The open-space area normally becomes a catch basin for activities that spill over from other areas. Whatever play originates in such an area quickly breaks up or gets out of hand. To supplement the open area, the types of boxes and props described above should be introduced.

What kind of space dominates your child's classroom? Is there much empty space or do tables and desks fill most of the room? How are props used in the classroom? Are they selected to support a specific play theme? How many big boxes or other private areas, such as closets, are used for activities? Are the boxes decorated to suggest different themes? How often are the boxes changed? For that matter, how often is the room's space reorganized?

DIARY:

TIME

Ask Erik the time at any hour of the day and invariably he'll say "something toward three." Three o'clock is the high point of Erik's day: it's when Christopher gets out of school.

Quiz him about when he goes to bed and you'll get, "after Batman," which translates to half-past seven. However, if the networks are running a two-hour "Batman" special, there's no way I can get Erik to bed before nine. You see, children measure time by events, not by clocks. And for our children, it's not time for sleep until the credits from their favorite TV show roll across the screen. As they do with the hours of their day, kids also mark off the year by big events—Halloween, Thanksgiving, Christmas, Valentine's Day, Easter, their birthdays, and so on. The only time they follow is that of their bodies' own internal clocks: they eat when they're hungry and play till the urge dies out.

At least, that's their routine at home. While in school they operate in another time zone. There, numbers aren't rounded off as in "something toward three." Instead the kids become like miniature sportscasters, rattling off times as if they were world records: "sand box, 8:46 to 9:16; art from 9:31 to 10:03, except on Friday when we paint with those messy sponges, then it's over at 10:07." Teachers and children both feel under pressure to cover certain pages by specific dates. Youngsters may also find that they can't be creative until 10:45 because that's when their class has the art room. Life in school seems to be a marathon against the clock. Interestingly, the term *curriculum* comes from a Latin word meaning "race."

Though schools today aren't organized like races, they do resemble other sports, namely, basketball, football, and hockey. All are divided into definite time periods and when the time runs out, the contest stops. The buzzer at the end of a basketball game is like the bell that rings at the end of the school day.

At home another game is being played. There the day is organized around innings. As in baseball, there are no time limits. To continue batting (or doing what one wants) one only has to avoid breaking the rules, which in baseball means that one must avoid making three outs, while at home it may mean that one must not become too noisy or knock over Daddy's drink. Innings, which are more open-ended, do more to stimulate creativity than do cut-and-dried periods. However, even a system of innings may have some drawbacks. A teacher may post assignments that are to be completed before the day ends, at the child's own pace, *but* in a particular order—for example, art, music, science, and so on. The child must do the assignments in the specified order. Other teachers allow "free substitution": the assignments still need be completed, but in any order and at the child's own speed.

Here are some different systems of organizing time, listed according to how well they support creative activity, with the most supportive listed first:

> Innings with free substitutions.
>
> Innings with no substitutions.
>
> Periods with free substitutions.
>
> Periods with no substitutions.

What system does your child's school use? Which do you use at home? Which one seems best for your youngster?

DIARY:
_____

PROPERTY

Around our neighborhood Erin was a regular tomboy. She really clicked with her brothers and their playmates. But at nursery school kids play by different rules: boys and girls do not mix.

After getting the cold shoulder for the umpteenth time, Erin finally attacked the problem head-on. She brought a few toys from home to bribe the boys to let her play. It worked like a charm. In no time at all she was running with the pack who only yesterday had snubbed her.

But these toys caused a bit of a stir with her teachers. In schools all property is public or shared and, as such, is under the control of the teacher. Privately owned toys cause teachers to lose some of their authority; they can't order the child to "let Joel play with *your* drum."

The presence of private property sets off a slight shift in the classroom's balance of power, and all teachers therefore have an ironclad law for dealing with it: "Leave your toy in the teacher's desk until show-and-tell." Show-and-tell is an interesting activity. It serves as a bridge between the child's private existence outside of school and her public life in school. It is during show-and-tell that kids often empty their pockets and their imaginations, as well.

Teachers appear to be in a bind. If they permit too many toys from home in school, they stand to lose control of the classroom; yet if they cut off this supply, they then run the risk of shutting off much of the creative inspiration that a youngster's personal effects and playthings provide.

There *is* a way out of this bind: teachers can bring in their own material from home. This practice is most common in classrooms where the teacher puts together homemade learning aids. Among other things, a teacher's preparation of such aids shows that the commercially available material doesn't fit every child's needs. When learning aids are tailored to various needs, there's a better chance that the children will use these materials creatively.

What follows is a scheme for evaluating the creative potential of various learning aids. They are arranged in order, starting with those that are the most creatively stimulating and ending with those that are the least stimulating.

Learing aids made by pupils and toys from home.

Learning aids made by teachers.

Converted learning aids. The teacher takes something that's not normally used for such instruction, such as a newspaper, and converts it to that purpose. For example, a teacher might use a newspaper to have pupils cut out letters that correspond to certain phonetic sounds.

Commercially prepared aids. These are the standard materials bought right off the shelves for mass consumption. They are all targeted at the "average" pupil and make little allowance for any individual differences. For that reason, their chance of triggering creativity in children is almost zero.

Where do the learning aids in your child's school fall in relationship to this scheme?

DIARY:

TEACHER'S ROLE

It happened at the local A & P somewhere between the Cocoa Puffs and Mrs. Paul's Fish Sticks, only to occur again in an unprecedented chain of events at the Laundromat. Outside of the time she saw a sleazy New York City Santa Claus staggering out of a 42nd Street peep show, I had never witnessed Erin so taken aback in her life.

In the course of no less than twenty minutes, Erin had seen her teacher, the real flesh-and-blood Mrs. Lambert, not only shopping but also washing her clothes. Who knows why, but seeing a teacher outside her usual turf spellbinds kids. Heaven forbid! Could teachers be like regular people? No way. Absolutely not! They're a special breed, set apart from the rest of us. They belong nowhere but in the classroom. Picturing them elsewhere is like thinking of a soldier abandoning his guard post.

It's hard to pinpoint why all kids hold this view. But observing a teacher—whom they see mainly as a public person—performing private duties is too much for most youngsters to handle.

Teachers maintain their public posture by distance. This is a "hands-off profession": kids are to be taught, not touched. Most teachers act like the "ugly American"—the tourist who never gets close to the natives. The only difference is that in the teacher's case the natives are all children. The touristlike teacher typically stays put in one area and, like a baseball pitcher on a mound, hurls out questions, answers, and orders, "Maryann, get off that window ledge, we're six stories up! Butch, what are you doing with that hammer over Phil's head?" Rarely does the tourist-teacher leave the mound, usually only to nail one or two children who have broken one of the teacher's pet rules. Under these circumstances, the culprits are usually manhandled.

A close cousin of the tourist is the talker. In this role, the teacher at least closes in on pupils, yet always stops short of an arm's reach.

Though the public roles of tourist and talker cover the main actions of a teacher, there are times when a teacher does step into the private roles of toucher and teaser. While it's easy to spot the toucher (gushing glad-handing, holding, and hugging are trademarks), this is not the most common private role that teachers adopt. When privacy is called for, most teachers carry on as teasers, draping themselves like umbrellas over the student (ever so careful never to make contact) of squatting so they can be eyeball-to-eyeball with the child. An experienced student of human nature once cracked that "the true measure of any teacher was whether she could squat or duck-walk for thirty seconds." Beyond its wit, there is a germ of truth in this observation. Perhaps a half a minute is just the amount of privacy that two people in a public situation, such as a classroom, can tolerate before things get too sticky or uneasy. And it may be precisely the right interval needed to spark the fuse that will ignite the child's wild imagination. Obviously different kids require different amounts of such intimate and personal attention from the teacher. Teachers can adjust their roles according to the needs of their pupils.

In trying to gauge the creative potential of a classroom, a good yardstick is the proportion of a day the teacher spends in these four roles:

1. Tourist: The teacher doesn't move around the room much and is usually at a considerable distance from the pupils with whom he or she is trying to communicate.
2. Talker: Though the teacher gets closer to the pupils, it's always within arm's length, and he or she lectures or dominates the exchange.
3. Teaser: The teacher surrounds or engulfs the pupil and neither does all the talking; if anything, communication is shared.
4. Toucher: The teacher "mixes it up" with pupils by holding and stroking them, all the while listening attentively to what they are saying.

Make a record of the time your child's teacher spends in these four roles.

DIARY:

CONCLUSION

Have you ever picked snow berries? Chances are you haven't unless you were born below the Mason-Dixon line and have seen King Cotton growing as Erik has. But even then these berries are hard to come by. Burpee's doesn't list them, nor is there any record of their taking root in any backyard gardens, save for those of a few individuals who still believe in Jack Frost, the Easter Bunny or the Bogeyman. You might be catching on at this point. A green thumb is of little help in cultivating snow berries. They are solely the product of Erik's wild and fertile imagination.

They first blossomed last Christmas when we were driving north to visit our relatives outside of Boston. Throughout the trip the weatherman kept promising "snow flurries" for December 25. And did he deliver—to the tune of about sixteen inches of snow flurries! Not only did Erik eat the white stuff and roll in it, but he also tried to save it by packing it into his pockets. He couldn't grasp the idea that the snow would melt. His only reaction was to go out and scoop up more snow, all the while muttering what we thought was "snow flurries." As it turned out, he was saying "snow berries." He thought snow grew out of the ground like cotton.

Why not? Being from the South he had never run into or experienced the word *flurries*. But it was close to something he knew quite well, *berries*. The connection was clear: white cotton grows from berries, so why not snow from snow berries?

By playing detective, I had figured out what Erik was thinking. Unfortunately I then dropped the ball and quickly became a dictionary: "Snow doesn't grow; it falls from the sky like other forms of precipitation, namely, rain, sleet, and hail." My definition really hit its mark. In two seconds Erik was out of the door, once more picking snow berries. Later in the day it snowed again, and Erik discovered for himself that snow berries don't grow. I wish I had been out with him then, filling my pockets with snow berries, rather than having wasted time trying to fill his head with my brand of logic.

Logic will come; it's part of growing up. Besides, the schools do a very good job of drumming it in, which is what one wants, but not at the expense of imagination. Fantasy is as much a part of our makeup as rationality and it hurts to see it let go. It's like losing an old friend; one wants to cry. Nothing captures this loss better than A.A. Milne's *House at Pooh Corner*. One day Christopher Robin is missing from the enchanted forest. He has left for school where he is to learn the three Rs. Eyoore is bitter and remarks scornfully, "Education." Eyoore has a right to feel this way because school has driven Christopher out of their make-believe Eden for good. Christopher will never return. Though the boy is easier to live with by adult standards, he has lost the look of the wide-eyed, wild dreamer. In short, he's no longer in love with his own thinking; with his mind now so busy with numbers, letters, and facts, there is no longer room for it.

Though we're all born with a certain amount of creativity that is supposed to last a lifetime, it rarely does last. As with many things in our lives, we don't appreciate creativity till it's gone. It comes so naturally when we're young that one can't conceive of its drying up. But it does. It's hard to picture that most of the bright and bubbly kids starting school today will be burnt out before they're forty or will at best remain daydreamers all their lives. Evidence of this is all around us. The President's Committee on Science and Technology recently told the National Academy of Engineers that American innovation and ingenuity are all but disappearing. Similar concerns are evident among social scientists. Dr. Robert Nesbet, dean of American sociology, and Professor Kenneth Boulding, past president of the American Economic Association, believe that today's complex human problems of living will never be solved unless our entire range of knowledge—instinctual and mystical, as well as rational—is brought to bear (Nesbet 1976; Silk 1976).

Don't scoff at these views. They're not just the pipe dreams of a couple of ivory tower bookworms. Such sentiments are echoed everyday in the hard-nosed world of business. Managers at IBM and at other giant corporations report that their day-to-day decision making is far too complex for rational analysis, so they rely on intuition and hunches (Mintzberg 1976).

Interestingly, as this book was being wrapped up and sent off to press the nation was preparing to celebrate the one hundredth birthday of one of the greatest minds of our times, if not of all times. So it seems only fitting that the reader be treated to what this man—Albert Einstein—held to be the key to his genius, "When I examine myself and my methods of thought, I come to the conclusion that the gift of fantasy has meant more to me than my talent for absorbing positive knowledge" (Stockton 1979).

Along with Albert Einstein, Christopher Robin, and my own Christopher, Erik, Erin, and Mary, let me wish you one and all a fantastic voyage back to the wonderful world of childhood where today can never be lost if you have a dream for tomorrow.

REFERENCES

BARRON, F. 1963. *Creativity and Personal Freedom.* Princeton, N.J.: Van Nostrand.

BURNHAM, E. 1892. "Individual Differences in the Imagination of Children." *Pedagogical Seminary* (1892):204-25.

COHEN, D. 1977. *Creativity: What Is It?* New York: M. Evans.

CROMBIE, A.C. 1952. *Augustine to Galileo,* 2nd. ed. Cambridge, Mass.: Harvard University Press.

ERIKSON, E. 1963. *Childhood and Society,* 2nd. ed. New York: W.W. Norton.

GETZEL, J., and P. JACKSON. 1962. *Creativity and Intelligence.* New York: John Wiley.

GHISELIN, B., ed. 1952. *The Creative Process.* Berkeley: University of California Press.

GORDON, W. 1961. *Synectics: The Development of Creative Capacities.* New York: Harper & Row.

HENDRICK, J. 1975. *The Whole Child.* St. Louis: C.V. Mosby.

HUGHES, H. 1963. "Individual and Group Creativity in Science." In *Essays on Creativity in Science.* M. Coles and H. Hughes, eds. New York: Harper & Row.

KAGAN, J. 1967. *Creativity and Intelligence.* Boston: Beacon Press.

KRIS, E. 1952. *Psychoanalytic Explorations in Art.* New York: International University Press.

KUBIE, L.S. 1958. *Neurotic Distortion of the Creative Process.* Lawrence: University of Kansas Press.

MINTZBERG, H. 1976. "The Manager's Job: Folklore and Fact." *Harvard Business Review* (1976).

NESBET, R. 1976. *Sociology as an Art Form.* New York: Oxford University Press.

PIAGET, J. 1926. *The Language and Thought of the Child.* New York: Harcourt, Brace.

———. 1928. *Judgment and Reasoning in the Child.* New York: Harcourt, Brace.

———. 1952. *The Origins of Intelligence in Children.* New York: International University Press.

SILK, L. 1976. *The Economist.* New York: Basic Books.

STOCKTON, W. 1979. "Celebrating Einstein." *New York Times Magazine,* February 18, 1979, p. 50.

TORRANCE, P. 1962. *Guiding Creativity and Talent.* Englewood Cliffs, N.J.: Prentice-Hall.

_____ . 1970. *Encouraging Creativity in the Classroom.* Dubuque, Iowa: William C. Brown.

WALLACH, M., and J. KAGAN. 1965. *Modes of Thinking in Young Children.* New York: Holt, Rinehart and Winston.

FURTHER READING

The Creative Child is a sequel to my earlier work, *Help Your Baby Learn.* Both works could stand as bookends between which you might want to read some of the following:

ARIETI, S. 1976. *Creativity: The Magic Synthesis.* New York: Basic Books.

BARREN F. 1961. *The Creative Personality.* Berkeley: University of California Press.

COHEN, D. 1977. *Creativity: What Is It?* New York: M. Evans.

FRAIBERG, S. 1959. *The Magic Years.* New York: Charles Scribner's.

GETZEL, J. and P. JACKSON. 1962. *Creativity and Intelligence.* New York: John Wiley.

GHISELIN, B. 1952. *The Creative Process.* Berkeley: University of California Press.

JONES, B. 1972. *Ethological Studies of Child Behavior.* New York: Cambridge University Press.

KOESTLER, A. 1964. *The Act of Creation.* New York: Macmillan.

MACKINNON, D., ed. 1961. *The Creative Person.* Berkeley: University of California Press.

MAY, R. 1976. *The Courage to Create.* New York: W.W. Norton.

MOONEY, R. and T. Razik, eds. 1967. *Explorations in Creativity.* New York: Harper & Row.

PIAGET, J. 1948. *The Moral Judgment of the Child.* New York: Free Press.

_____ . 1951. *The Child's Concept of the World.* Atlantic Highlands, N.J. Humanities Press.

_____ . 1962. *Play Dreams and Imitation in Children.* New York: W.W. Norton.

INDEX